W9-BLJ-191

Quick Scripture Reference for Counseling

THIRD EDITION

JOHN G. KRUIS

Baker Books

A Division of Baker Book House Co
Grand Rapids, Michigan 49516

© 1988, 1994, 2000 by John G. Kruis

Published by Baker Books
a division of Baker Book House Company
P.O. Box 6287, Grand Rapids, MI 49516-6287

Seventh printing, February 2005

Printed in the United States of America

ISBN 0-8010-9102-0

For current information about all releases from Baker Book House, visit our web site:
http://www.bakerbooks.com

Compiled for ...

your personal benefit, and to help you use the Scriptures more effectively in counseling.

Dedicated to ...

my wife, Gene, my devoted helper, "a wife of noble character ... a woman who fears the LORD" (Prov. 31:10, 30), the dedicated mother of our five children: Ronald, John, Nelva, Kevin, and David.

All Scripture is God-breathed and is useful for teaching, rebuking, correcting and training in righteousness, so that the man of God may be thoroughly equipped for every good work.

2 Timothy 3:16–17

Subject Guide

5

Salvation

Leading a Person to Christ

 I. Apart from Christ we are helpless and sinful.
   A. We are all sinners.
   B. We are in spiritual bondage.
   C. We are alienated from God.
   D. Knowledge of sin comes by the law of God.
   E. God, in his justice, punishes sinners.
   F. We cannot save ourselves in any way.
 II. Jesus saves us by grace and through faith.
   A. Jesus suffered and died for sinners.
   B. Examples of those who were saved by grace and through faith.
 III. The Lord calls sinners like you and me.
 IV. We are saved to joyfully obey and serve the Lord.

Introduction

Why This Book?

For Biblical Counseling

"All Scripture is God-breathed and is useful for teaching, rebuking, correcting and training in righteousness, so that the man of God may be thoroughly equipped for every good work" (2 Tim. 3:16–17). "The word of God is living and active. Sharper than any double-edged sword, it penetrates even to dividing soul and spirit, joints and marrow; it judges the thoughts and attitudes of the heart" (Heb. 4:12).

As you do the Lord's work, the Holy Spirit is always the primary counselor, and he works powerfully, sovereignly through his own Word. He brings people to a conviction of sin and to a saving knowledge of Jesus Christ through his Word. It is by the Scriptures that he teaches them how to love God and their neighbors as themselves, to live a life of faith and obedience in response to his saving grace. Through the Scriptures the Holy Spirit comforts, rebukes, corrects, and trains them in righteousness. In this way people of all ages and from various walks of life are helped; all kinds of personal, marriage and family problems are resolved—and God is glorified.

It is, therefore, essential for you to be "thoroughly equipped" with the Scriptures, prepared for "every good work." The better equipped you are, the more effective you will be in helping others.

For Personal, Marriage, and Family Needs

This *Quick Scripture Reference for Counseling* was first published in March of 1988. As the third edition goes to press over 175,000 copies of the English edition have been sold internationally. It has become evident that it is being used for much more than counseling. Many are using the book to help meet their personal, marriage, and family needs, including resolving conflicts within the home. Some are using it as a guide for personal and family devotions.

The Uniqueness of This Book

This *Quick Scripture Reference for Counseling* is designed especially to help God's people use the Scriptures more effectively in their counseling ministries. It has several distinctive features. Scripture passages and texts are listed under topics. They are arranged so that you can see at a glance the gist and the significance of each text or passage as it relates to the topic under which it is listed. In many instances Bible verses are quoted in their entirety so that you have them immediately before you. When longer passages are listed, often the key verses are quoted.

To maximize the usefulness of the book the entries under each topic have been numbered so that, as you prepare an agenda for counseling someone, you can easily list several pertinent Bible passages to have right at your fingertips. For example, as you seek to lead a person to the forgiveness of sins, or assurance, you might write on your agenda something like this:

Forgiveness of sins—page 72
1. Believers are made as white as snow. Isa. 1:18.
6. God will not despise a broken spirit and a contrite heart. Ps. 51:17.
9. God calls sinners to seek him and promises them forgiveness when they repent. Isa. 55:6–7.
11. Jesus forgave the penitent woman. Luke 7:36–50.
26. God has lavished his grace on us, choosing us, forgiving us of all our sins through the shed blood of Christ. Eph. 1:3-10.

This feature will also help you to prepare homework assignments that meet the specific needs of each counselee.

My prayer is that this book will help many to use the Scriptures more effectively in counseling others, for their comfort, joy, peace, and eternal well-being, and above all for God's glory.

Adultery

If one continues to live in the state of adultery, see also Sexual Immorality, p. 177; Warnings, p. 192; and Obedience, p. 111. If one repents of adultery, see Forgiveness of Sins, p. 72; and Peace, p. 122.

1. Adultery is out of the heart.

   Matt. 15:19. Out of the heart come evil thoughts, murder, adultery, sexual immorality, theft, false testimony, slander.

2. No adulterers go to heaven.

   1 Cor. 6:9–10. Do you not know that the wicked will not inherit the kingdom of God? Do not be deceived: Neither the sexually immoral, nor idolaters nor adulterers nor male prostitutes nor homosexual offenders nor thieves nor the greedy nor drunkards nor slanderers nor swindlers will inherit the kingdom of God.

3. God will judge the adulterer.

   Heb. 13:4. Marriage should be honored by all, and the marriage bed kept pure, for God will judge the adulterer and all the sexually immoral.

4. Adultery can be avoided.

   Prov. 4:23. Above all else, guard your heart, for it is the wellspring of life.
   Prov. 4:13–27. *(Stay far from the path of evil.)*
   Prov. 6:27–28. *(Don't play with fire.)* Can a man scoop fire into his lap without his clothes being burned? Can a man walk on hot coals without his feet being scorched?

5. Shun adultery.

   Prov. 6:20–35.

6. **The adulteress' snare leads to misery.**

    Prov. 7:1–27.

7. **The adulteress' snare is a deep pit.**

    Prov. 22:14. The mouth of an adulteress is a deep pit; he who is under the LORD's wrath will fall into it.

8. **David fed the flame.**

    2 Sam. 11:2–3. One evening David got up from his bed and walked around on the roof of the palace. From the roof he saw a woman bathing. The woman was very beautiful, and David sent someone to find out about her.

9. **David was depressed before he confessed his sin of adultery.**

    Ps. 32:3–5.

10. **Nathan called David to repent of his adultery.**

    2 Sam. 12:1–14. *(The prophet Nathan spoke to David in a parable after he had sinned with Bathsheba.)*

11. **David confessed his adultery, and God graciously forgave him.**

    Ps. 32; Ps. 51. *(David pleaded for God's forgiveness and expressed his joy after being forgiven.)*

12. **God forgives the sin of adultery and frees the sinner from it.**

    1 Cor. 6:11. That [adulterers, etc.] is what some of you were. But you were washed, you were sanctified, you were justified in the name of the Lord Jesus Christ and by the Spirit of our God.

13. **Looking on a woman lustfully is adultery; spiritual surgery is needed.**

    Matt. 5:27–30. You have heard that it was said, "Do not commit adultery." But I tell you that anyone who looks at a woman lustfully has already committed adultery with her in his heart. If your right eye causes you to sin, gouge it out and throw it away. It is better for you to lose one part of your body than for your whole body to be thrown into hell. And if your right hand causes you to sin, cut it off and throw it away. It is better for you to lose one part of your body than for your whole body to go into hell.

14. **Beware of seductive women.**

    Prov. 23:26–28. My son, give me your heart and let your eyes keep to my ways, for a prostitute is a deep pit and a wayward wife is a narrow well. Like a bandit she lies in wait, and multiplies the unfaithful among men.

15. Stolen water is sweet, but . . .

Prov. 9:17–18. "Stolen water is sweet; food eaten in secret is delicious!" But little do they know that the dead are there, that her guests are in the depths of the grave.

16. Keep the seventh commandment.

Exod. 20:14. You shall not commit adultery.

17. Anyone who marries a wrongfully divorced person commits adultery.

Matt. 5:31–32. "It has been said, 'Anyone who divorces his wife must give her a certificate of divorce.' But I tell you that anyone who divorces his wife, except for marital unfaithfulness, causes her to commit adultery, and anyone who marries a woman so divorced commits adultery."

18. Anyone who divorces his or her spouse for any reason other than adultery and marries another commits adultery.

Matt. 19:9. I tell you that anyone who divorces his wife, except for marital unfaithfulness, and marries another woman commits adultery.

Rom. 7:2–3. For example, by law a married woman is bound to her husband as long as he is alive, but if her husband dies, she is released from the law of marriage. So then, if she marries another man while her husband is still alive, she is called an adulteress. But if her husband dies, she is released from that law and is not an adulteress, even though she marries another man.

19. When he was tempted by Potiphar's wife to commit adultery, Joseph refused to sin against God.

Gen. 39:6–20.

Gen. 39:9–10. "How then could I do such a wicked thing and sin against God?" And though she spoke to Joseph day after day, he refused to go to bed with her or even be with her.

Affliction, Discipline, Chastisement, Trials

See also Comfort, p. 37; Prayer, p. 137; and Trust, p. 186.

1. **Not all affliction is for specific sins. God often sends affliction to purify and strengthen our faith, for his glory.**

   1 Peter 1:6–7. In this you greatly rejoice, though now for a little while you may have had to suffer grief in all kinds of trials. These have come so that your faith—of greater worth than gold, which perishes even though refined by fire—may be proved genuine and may result in praise, glory and honor when Jesus Christ is revealed.

   John 9:1–3. As he went along, he saw a man blind from birth. His disciples asked him, "Rabbi, who sinned, this man or his parents, that he was born blind?" "Neither this man nor his parents sinned," said Jesus, "but this happened so that the work of God might be displayed in his life."

2. **Job, a godly man, was severely tried; he lost his possessions and his children.**

   Job 1:1–22.

   Job 1:1. In the land of Uz there lived a man whose name was Job. This man was blameless and upright; he feared God and shunned evil.

   Job 1:8. Then the LORD said to Satan, "Have you considered my servant Job? There is no one on earth like him; he is blameless and upright, a man who fears God and shuns evil."

3. **Job did not get angry at God (which would have been a sinful reaction). Rather, he accepted it by faith and worshiped him.**

Job 1:20–22. At this, Job got up and tore his robe and shaved his head. Then he fell to the ground in worship and said: "Naked I came from my mother's womb, and naked I will depart. The LORD gave and the LORD has taken away; may the name of the LORD be praised." In all this, Job did not sin by charging God with wrongdoing.

4. God at times sends trials to develop patience in us.

James 1:2–4. Consider it pure joy, my brothers, whenever you face trials of many kinds, because you know that the testing of your faith develops perseverance. Perseverance must finish its work so that you may be mature and complete, not lacking anything.

5. The psalmist was thankful for affliction, for it taught him to keep God's precepts.

Ps. 119:67–68. Before I was afflicted I went astray, but now I obey your word. You are good, and what you do is good; teach me your decrees.

Ps. 119:71–72. It was good for me to be afflicted so that I might learn your decrees. The law from your mouth is more precious to me than thousands of pieces of silver and gold.

Ps. 119:75–76. I know, O LORD, that your laws are righteous, and in faithfulness you have afflicted me. May your unfailing love be my comfort, according to your promise to your servant.

6. We must neither make light of God's discipline nor lose heart because of it.

Heb. 12:5–6. And you have forgotten that word of encouragement that addresses you as sons: "My son, do not make light of the Lord's discipline, and do not lose heart when he rebukes you, because the Lord disciplines those he loves, and he punishes everyone he accepts as a son."

7. God disciplines his children to promote sanctification.

Heb. 12:5–11.

Heb. 12:10–11. Our fathers disciplined us for a little while as they thought best; but God disciplines us for our good, that we may share in his holiness. No discipline seems pleasant at the time, but painful. Later on, however, it produces a harvest of righteousness and peace for those who have been trained by it.

8. **God disciplined and tried his people on their journey to the promised land to teach them important lessons.**

    Deut. 8:2–5. Remember how the LORD your God led you all the way in the desert these forty years, to humble you and to test you in order to know what was in your heart, whether or not you would keep his commands. He humbled you, causing you to hunger and then feeding you with manna, which neither you nor your fathers had known, to teach you that man does not live on bread alone but on every word that comes from the mouth of the LORD. Your clothes did not wear out and your feet did not swell during these forty years. Know then in your heart that as a man disciplines his son, so the LORD your God disciplines you.

9. **God tried his people at Marah, where he turned the bitter water sweet and soon gave a time of refreshment at Elim.**

    Exod. 15:22–27.
    Exod. 15:25. Then Moses cried out to the LORD, and the LORD showed him a piece of wood. He threw it into the water, and the water became sweet. There the LORD made a decree and a law for them, and there he tested them.
    Exod. 15:27. Then they came to Elim, where there were twelve springs and seventy palm trees, and they camped there near the water.

10. **To the lukewarm church Jesus declares that he rebukes and disciplines those whom he loves.**

    Rev. 3:14–22. *(the letter to the church at Laodicea)*
    Rev. 3:19–20. "Those whom I love I rebuke and discipline. So be earnest, and repent. Here I am! I stand at the door and knock. If anyone hears my voice and opens the door, I will come in and eat with him, and he with me."

11. **Paul was given a thorn in the flesh, a continual affliction to bear. God promised him that his grace would always be sufficient.**

    2 Cor. 12:7–10. To keep me from becoming conceited because of these surpassingly great revelations, there was given me a thorn in my flesh, a messenger of Satan, to torment me. Three times I pleaded with the Lord to take it away from me. But he said to me, "My grace is sufficient for you, for my power is made perfect in weakness." Therefore I will boast all the more gladly about my weaknesses, so that Christ's power may rest on me. That is why, for Christ's sake, I delight in weaknesses, in insults, in hardships, in persecutions, in difficulties. For when I am weak, then I am strong.

12. In everything God works for the good of those who love him.

Rom. 8:28. We know that in all things God works for the good of those who love him, who have been called according to his purpose.

13. God will never give you more than you can bear.

1 Cor. 10:13. No temptation has seized you except what is common to man. And God is faithful; he will not let you be tempted beyond what you can bear. But when you are tempted, he will also provide a way out so that you can stand up under it.

14. We cannot always comprehend God's ways, as he, in his wisdom, carries out his plan.

Rom. 11:33–36. Oh, the depth of the riches of the wisdom and knowledge of God! How unsearchable his judgments, and his paths beyond tracing out! "Who has known the mind of the Lord? Or who has been his counselor?" "Who has ever given to God, that God should repay him?" For from him and through him and to him are all things. To him be the glory forever! Amen.

15. King Hezekiah praised God for his loving discipline.

Isa. 38:15–19.

Isa. 38:15. But what can I say? He has spoken to me, and he himself has done this. I will walk humbly all my years because of this anguish of my soul.

Isa. 38:17. Surely it was for my benefit that I suffered such anguish. In your love you kept me from the pit of destruction; you have put all my sins behind your back.

16. We can rejoice in our sufferings, which produce perseverance.

Rom. 5:3. We also rejoice in our sufferings, because we know that suffering produces perseverance; perseverance, character; and character, hope.

James 1:2–4. Consider it pure joy, my brothers, whenever you face trials of many kinds, because you know that the testing of your faith develops perseverance. Perseverance must finish its work so that you may be mature and complete, not lacking anything.

17. God blesses those who persevere under trials.

James 1:12. Blessed is the man who perseveres under trial, because when he has stood the test, he will receive the crown of life that God has promised to those who love him.

18. Our present sufferings are not worth comparing with the glory that will be revealed in us.

Rom. 8:18. I consider that our present sufferings are not worth comparing with the glory that will be revealed in us.

19. Paul says that he suffered under great stress so that he might learn to rely more on God.

2 Cor. 1:8–9. We do not want to be uninformed, brothers, about the hardships we suffered in the province of Asia. We were under great pressure, far beyond our ability to endure, so that we despaired even of life. Indeed, in our hearts we felt the sentence of death. But this happened that we might not rely on ourselves but on God, who raises the dead.

20. Paul says that God always has and always will deliver him.

2 Cor. 1:10–11. He has delivered us from such a deadly peril, and he will deliver us. On him we have set our hope that he will continue to deliver us, as you help us by your prayers. Then many will give thanks on our behalf for the gracious favor granted us in answer to the prayers of many.

21. At times God gives us trials so that our faith may be purified as gold is refined by fire, that Christ may be honored and glorified.

1 Peter 1:7–8. These [all kinds of trials] have come so that your faith—of greater worth than gold, which perishes even though refined by fire—may be proved genuine and may result in praise, glory and honor when Jesus Christ is revealed. Though you have not seen him, you love him; and even though you do not see him now, you believe in him and are filled with an inexpressible and glorious joy.

22. In the time of trouble you can experience God's protective care and, even through the tears, sing praises to God.

Ps. 27:5–6. For on the day of trouble he will keep me safe in his dwelling; he will hide me in the shelter of his tabernacle and set me high upon a rock. Then my head will be exalted above the enemies who surround me; at his tabernacle will I sacrifice with shouts of joy; I will sing and make music to the LORD.

23. Paul and Silas were singing praises to God while they were suffering severely for the sake of the gospel.

> Acts 16:16–28. *(Paul and Silas were severely flogged, thrown into prison, and their feet were fastened in stocks.)*

> Acts 16:25. About midnight Paul and Silas were praying and singing hymns to God, and the other prisoners were listening to them.

24. While he was suffering in prison at Rome, Paul rejoiced over what God was accomplishing through it all.

> Phil. 1:12–26.

> Phil. 1:12–14. Now I want you to know, brothers, that what has happened to me has really served to advance the gospel. As a result, it has become clear throughout the whole palace guard and to everyone else that I am in chains for Christ. Because of my chains, most of the brothers in the Lord have been encouraged to preach the word of God more courageously and fearlessly.

25. Although Paul suffered in many ways, he did not lose heart. God kept strengthening him day by day, and he looked forward to his eternal reward.

> 2 Cor. 4:8–18.

> 2 Cor. 4:16–18. Therefore we do not lose heart. Though outwardly we are wasting away, yet inwardly we are being renewed day by day. For our light and momentary troubles are achieving for us an eternal glory that far outweighs them all. So we fix our eyes not on what is seen, but on what is unseen. For what is seen is temporary, but what is unseen is eternal.

For more on how to handle affliction see Comfort, p. 37; Death, Eternal Life, p. 51; Prayer, p. 137; Providence of God, p. 146; Trust, p. 186.

Alcohol, Drug Abuse

See also Overcoming Sin, p. 117.

1. **Your body is a temple of the Holy Spirit.**

    1 Cor. 6:15. Do you not know that your bodies are members of Christ himself?

    1 Cor. 6:19–20. Do you not know that your body is a temple of the Holy Spirit, who is in you, whom you have received from God? You are not your own; you were bought at a price. Therefore honor God with your body.

2. **Jesus warns against the abuse of alcohol.**

    Luke 21:34. Be careful, or your hearts will be weighed down with dissipation, drunkenness and the anxieties of life, and that day will close on you unexpectedly like a trap.

3. **Wine is a mocker, beer a brawler.**

    Prov. 20:1. Wine is a mocker and beer a brawler; whoever is led astray by them is not wise.

4. **Don't love wine.**

    Prov. 21:17. He who loves pleasure will become poor; whoever loves wine and oil will never be rich.

5. **Heavy drinking brings misery.**

    Prov. 23:29–35.

6. **Consider the sad picture of a drunkard. (The Bible tells it like it is!)**

    Prov. 23:32–35.

7. **God's wrath was upon Israel for its sin of drunkenness.**

    Isa. 28:1–4.

8. **Isaiah gives us a vivid picture of a drunk losing his moral judgment.**

    Isa. 28:7–8. These also stagger from wine and reel from beer: Priests and prophets stagger from beer and are befuddled with wine; they reel from beer, they stagger when seeing visions, they stumble when rendering decisions. All the tables are covered with vomit and there is not a spot without filth.

9. **Paul gives us a timely warning and instruction.**

    Eph. 5:15–18. Be very careful, then, how you live—not as unwise but as wise, making the most of every opportunity, because the days are evil. Therefore do not be foolish, but understand what the Lord's will is. Do not get drunk on wine, which leads to debauchery. Instead, be filled with the Spirit.

10. **Drunkenness breaks down morals.**

    Gen. 9:20–23. *(the example of Noah)*
    Gen. 19:30–38. *(the example of Lot)*

11. **No drunkard shall enter heaven.**

    1 Cor. 6:9–10. Do you not know that the wicked will not inherit the kingdom of God? Do not be deceived: Neither the sexually immoral . . . nor drunkards . . . will inherit the kingdom of God.

12. **One can be saved from drunkenness and set free.**

    1 Cor. 6:11. That [drunkards, etc.] is what some of you were. But you were washed, you were sanctified, you were justified in the name of the Lord Jesus Christ and by the Spirit of our God.

13. **Don't associate with drunkards.**

    1 Cor. 5:11. Now I am writing you that you must not associate with anyone who calls himself a brother but is sexually immoral or greedy, an idolater or a slanderer, a drunkard or a swindler. With such a man do not even eat.

14. **Be wise! Don't join those who abuse alcohol.**

    Prov. 23:19–20. Listen, my son, and be wise, and keep your heart on the right path. Do not join those who drink too much wine or gorge themselves on meat.

Anger, Hot Temper

For help in overcoming uncontrolled anger and a hot temper, see Overcoming Sin, p. 117; Progressive Sanctification, p. 141; and Self-control, p. 171.

1. Anger is not in itself sinful.

> **Ps. 7:11.** *(God is angry with the wicked.)*
> **1 Kings 11:9.** *(God was angry with Solomon.)*
> **2 Kings 17:18.** *(God was angry with Israel.)*
> **Mark 3:5.** *(Jesus was angry with the Pharisees.)*

2. Be slow to become angry.

> **Prov. 14:16–17.** A wise man fears the LORD and shuns evil, but a fool is hotheaded and reckless. A quick-tempered man does foolish things, and a crafty man is hated.
>
> **Prov. 14:29.** A patient man has great understanding, but a quick-tempered man displays folly.
>
> **James 1:19–20.** My dear brothers, take note of this: Everyone should be quick to listen, slow to speak and slow to become angry, for man's anger does not bring about the righteous life that God desires.

3. Love covers a multitude of sins and overlooks many offenses.

> **Prov. 10:12.** Hatred stirs up dissension, but love covers over all wrongs.
>
> **Prov. 12:16.** A fool shows his annoyance at once, but a prudent man overlooks an insult.
>
> **Prov. 17:9.** He who covers over an offense promotes love, but whoever repeats the matter separates close friends.

Prov. 19:11. A man's wisdom gives him patience; it is to his glory to overlook an offense.

1 Peter 4:8. Above all, love each other deeply, because love covers over a multitude of sins.

4. Seek the way of love.

1 Cor. 13:4–5. Love is patient, love is kind. It is not easily angered.

5. Cain's anger turned into hate and murder.

Gen. 4:3–8.

Gen. 4:4. But Abel brought fat portions from some of the first-born of his flock. The LORD looked with favor on Abel and his offering.

Gen. 4:8. Now Cain said to his brother Abel, "Let's go out to the field." And while they were in the field, Cain attacked his brother Abel and killed him.

6. Hot words stir up strife.

Prov. 15:1. A gentle answer turns away wrath, but a harsh word stirs up anger.

7. A hot-tempered man creates dissension.

Prov. 15:18. A hot-tempered man stirs up dissension, but a patient man calms a quarrel.

8. Do not associate with a hot-tempered man.

Prov. 22:24–25. Do not make friends with a hot-tempered man, do not associate with one easily angered, or you may learn his ways and get yourself ensnared.

9. Control yourself.

Prov. 25:28. Like a city whose walls are broken down is a man who lacks self-control.

Prov. 29:22. An angry man stirs up dissension, and a hot-tempered one commits many sins.

Prov. 30:33. For as churning the milk produces butter, and as twisting the nose produces blood, so stirring up anger produces strife.

10. Fits of rage belong to your sinful nature, the way of sin.

Gal. 5:19–21.

11. **Good news! Through the Spirit you can overcome the sin of a hot temper.**

    Gal. 5:22–25. But the fruit of the Spirit is love, joy, peace, patience, kindness, goodness, faithfulness, gentleness and self-control. Against such things there is no law. Those who belong to Christ Jesus have crucified the sinful nature with its passions and desires. Since we live by the Spirit, let us keep in step with the Spirit.

    Col. 3:8. But now you must rid yourselves of all such things as these: anger, rage, malice, slander, and filthy language from your lips.

12. **Handle anger in a godly way. Do not let the sun go down on your anger.**

    Eph. 4:26. "In your anger do not sin." Do not let the sun go down while you are still angry.

13. **Jesus said that one who is angry with his brother without a cause will be subject to judgment.**

    Matt. 5:21–22. "You have heard that it was said to the people long ago, 'Do not murder, and anyone who murders will be subject to judgment.' But I tell you that anyone who is angry with his brother will be subject to judgment. Again, anyone who says to his brother, 'Raca,' is answerable to the Sanhedrin. But anyone who says, 'You fool!' will be in danger of the fire of hell."

Assurance
(of Salvation)

1. Job had assurance.

Job 19:25–27. I know that my Redeemer lives, and that in the end he will stand upon the earth. And after my skin has been destroyed, yet in my flesh I will see God; I myself will see him with my own eyes—I, and not another. How my heart yearns within me!

2. The Spirit testifies with our spirit.

Rom. 8:16–17. The Spirit himself testifies with our spirit that we are God's children. Now if we are children, then we are heirs—heirs of God and co-heirs with Christ, if indeed we share in his sufferings in order that we may also share in his glory.

3. We know that we live in him; we know and rely on the love God has for us.

1 John 4:13–16. We know that we live in him and he in us because he has given us of his Spirit. And we have seen and testify that the Father has sent his Son to be the Savior of the world. If anyone acknowledges that Jesus is the Son of God, God lives in him and he in God. And so we know and rely on the love God has for us.

4. You may know that you have eternal life.

1 John 5:13. I write these things to you who believe in the name of the Son of God so that you may know that you have eternal life.

5. Paul had assurance of eternal life.

2 Tim. 1:12. I know whom I have believed, and am convinced that he is able to guard what I have entrusted to him for that day.

6. Now we are the children of God, and we shall be like him.

1 John 3:1–3. How great is the love the Father has lavished on us, that we should be called children of God! And that is what we are! The reason the world does not know us is that it did not know him. Dear friends, now we are children of God, and what we will be has not yet been made known. But we know that when he appears, we shall be like him, for we shall see him as he is. Everyone who has this hope in him purifies himself, just as he is pure.

7. A Christian has a living hope through Christ's resurrection.

1 Peter 1:3–5. Praise be to the God and Father of our Lord Jesus Christ! In his great mercy he has given us new birth into a living hope through the resurrection of Jesus Christ from the dead, and into an inheritance that can never perish, spoil or fade—kept in heaven for you, who through faith are shielded by God's power until the coming of the salvation that is ready to be revealed in the last time.

Bitterness, Resentment, Hate

1. **In the power of the Holy Spirit every Christian can and must get rid of bitterness and hatred and become a kind, compassionate, forgiving person.**

   Eph. 4:31–32. Get rid of all bitterness, rage and anger, brawling and slander, along with every form of malice. Be kind and compassionate to one another, forgiving each other, just as in Christ God forgave you.

2. **Quit biting and devouring each other.**

   Gal. 5:15. If you keep on biting and devouring each other, watch out or you will be destroyed by each other.

3. **Bitterness belongs to the sinful nature.**

   Gal. 5:19. The acts of the sinful nature are obvious: . . . discord, jealousy, fits of rage, selfish ambition, dissensions, factions . . . and the like.

4. **Let no bitter root grow.**

   Heb. 12:15. See to it that no one misses the grace of God and that no bitter root grows up to cause trouble and defile many.

5. **Joseph's brothers allowed bitterness to grow into hatred and murder in the heart.**

   Gen. 37.

6. **Cain's anger turned to bitterness, hatred, and murder.**

   Gen. 4:3–8.

7. **Hatred is forbidden.**

   Lev. 19:16–17. "Do not go about spreading slander among your people. Do not do anything that endangers your neighbor's life. I am the LORD. Do not hate your brother in your heart. Rebuke your neighbor frankly so that you will not share in his guilt."

8. One who hates lives in darkness.

1 John 2:9–11. Anyone who claims to be in the light but hates his brother is still in the darkness. Whoever loves his brother lives in the light, and there is nothing in him to make him stumble. But whoever hates his brother is in the darkness and walks around in the darkness; he does not know where he is going, because the darkness has blinded him.

9. The way of a malicious man is deceitful.

Prov. 26:24–26. A malicious man disguises himself with his lips, but in his heart he harbors deceit. Though his speech is charming, do not believe him, for seven abominations fill his heart. His malice may be concealed by deception, but his wickedness will be exposed in the assembly.

10. Hatred is murder.

1 John 3:11–20.

1 John 3:15. Anyone who hates his brother is a murderer, and you know that no murderer has eternal life in him.

11. Jesus commands us not to hate our enemies, but love them and pray for them.

Matt. 5:43–48.

12. If you claim to love God but you hate your brother, you are a liar.

1 John 4:20–21. If anyone says, "I love God," yet hates his brother, he is a liar. For anyone who does not love his brother, whom he has seen, cannot love God, whom he has not seen. And he has given us this command: Whoever loves God must also love his brother.

13. To conceal or harbor hatred in your heart is lying before the face of God.

Prov. 10:18. He who conceals his hatred has lying lips, and whoever spreads slander is a fool.

14. Hatred stirs up dissension.

Prov. 10:12. Hatred stirs up dissension, but love covers all wrongs.

Blame Shifting

1. **Adam and Eve tried to shift blame.**

    Gen. 3:12–13. The man said, "The woman you put here with me—she gave me some fruit from the tree, and I ate it." Then the LORD God said to the woman, "What is this you have done?" The woman said, "The serpent deceived me, and I ate."

2. **Some try to blame God.**

    Prov. 19:3. A man's own folly ruins his life, yet his heart rages against the LORD.

3. **Do not judge others while you fail to acknowledge your own sin.**

    Matt. 7:1–5. Do not judge, or you too will be judged. For in the same way you judge others, you will be judged, and with the measure you use, it will be measured to you. Why do you look at the speck of sawdust in your brother's eye and pay no attention to the plank in your own eye? How can you say to your brother, "Let me take the speck out of your eye," when all the time there is a plank in your own eye? You hypocrite, first take the plank out of your own eye, and then you will see clearly to remove the speck from your brother's eye.

Children

See also Training Children, p. 182; and Youth, p. 204.

1. **Children belong first to God and are his gift to us.**

   Ps. 127:3–5.

   Ps. 127:3. Sons are a heritage from the LORD, children a reward from him.

2. **Children of believers belong to God and are in his covenant.**

   Gen. 17:7. I will establish my covenant as an everlasting covenant between me and you and your descendants after you for the generations to come, to be your God and the God of your descendants after you.

   Acts 2:39. The promise is for you and your children and for all who are far off—for all whom the Lord our God will call.

3. **God delights in the praise and worship of children.**

   Ps. 8:2. From the lips of children and infants you have ordained praise because of your enemies, to silence the foe and the avenger.

4. **Jesus accepted the praise of children.**

   Matt. 21:15–16. When the chief priests and the teachers of the law saw the wonderful things he did and the children shouting in the temple area, "Hosanna to the Son of David," they were indignant. "Do you hear what these children are saying?" they asked him. "Yes," replied Jesus, "have you never read, 'From the lips of children and infants you have ordained praise'?"

5. **Jesus loves little children; of such is God's kingdom.**

   Matt. 19:13–15. Then little children were brought to Jesus for him to place his hands on them and pray for them. But the disciples rebuked those who brought them. Jesus said, "Let the little children come to me, and do not hinder them, for the kingdom of heaven belongs to such as these." When he had placed his hands on them, he went on from there.

6. **David was comforted by the knowledge that his infant son went to heaven when he died, and that he would see him there.**

   2 Sam. 12:18–23.

   2 Sam. 12:23. Now that he is dead, why should I fast? Can I bring him back again? I will go to him, but he will not return to me.

Church, Communion of Saints

See also Loving and Serving Others, p. 96; and Church Discipline, p. 35.

1. **The church is one.**

    Eph. 4:3–6. Make every effort to keep the unity of the Spirit through the bond of peace. There is one body and one Spirit—just as you were called to one hope when you were called—one Lord, one faith, one baptism; one God and Father of all, who is over all and through all and in all.

2. **The church is one body with many functions; each member has a purpose.**

    Rom. 12:4–8. Just as each of us has one body with many members, and these members do not all have the same function, so in Christ we who are many form one body, and each member belongs to all the others. We have different gifts, according to the grace given us. If a man's gift is prophesying, let him use it in proportion to his faith. If it is serving, let him serve; if it is teaching, let him teach; if it is encouraging, let him encourage; if it is contributing to the needs of others, let him give generously; if it is leadership, let him govern diligently; if it is showing mercy, let him do it cheerfully.

3. **Together, Christians constitute God's household, in which he lives by his Spirit.**

    Eph. 2:19–22. You are no longer foreigners and aliens, but fellow citizens with God's people and members of God's household, built on the foundation of the apostles and prophets, with Christ Jesus himself as the chief cornerstone. In him the whole building is joined together and rises to become a holy temple in the Lord. And in him you too are being built together to become a dwelling in which God lives by his Spirit.

4. **Keep the unity of believers; don't follow men, but Christ.**
   1 Cor. 1:10–17.
   1 Cor. 1:11–13. My brothers, some from Chloe's household have informed me that there are quarrels among you. What I mean is this: One of you says, "I follow Paul"; another, "I follow Apollos"; another, "I follow Cephas"; still another, "I follow Christ." Is Christ divided? Was Paul crucified for you? Were you baptized into the name of Paul?

5. **Gifts of the Spirit differ. Each member must use his or her gifts to serve others.**
   Eph. 4:11–13. It was he who gave some to be apostles, some to be prophets, some to be evangelists, and some to be pastors and teachers, to prepare God's people for works of service, so that the body of Christ may be built up until we all reach unity in the faith and in the knowledge of the Son of God and become mature, attaining to the whole measure of the fullness of Christ.
   1 Cor. 12:1–11.
   1 Cor. 12:4–7. There are different kinds of gifts, but the same Spirit. There are different kinds of service, but the same Lord. There are different kinds of working, but the same God works all of them in all men. Now to each one the manifestation of the Spirit is given for the common good.

6. **Each member of the body is necessary. We need one another. All must have a deep concern for each other.**
   1 Cor. 12:12–31.
   1 Cor. 12:25–26. . . . so that there should be no division in the body, but that its parts should have equal concern for each other. If one part suffers, every part suffers with it; if one part is honored, every part rejoices with it.

7. **Christ is the head of the church, his body.**
   Eph. 1:20–23.

Eph. 1:22–23. God placed all things under his feet and appointed him to be head over everything for the church, which is his body, the fullness of him who fills everything in every way.

Eph. 5:23. For the husband is the head of the wife as Christ is the head of the church, his body, of which he is the Savior.

8. **Christ loves the church.**

Eph. 5:25. Husbands, love your wives, just as Christ loved the church and gave himself up for her. . . .

9. **Attend worship services faithfully.**

Heb. 10:25. Let us not give up meeting together, as some are in the habit of doing, but let us encourage one another—and all the more as you see the Day approaching.

10. **The psalmist longed to be in the house of God.**

Ps. 84.

Ps. 84:1–2. How lovely is your dwelling place, O LORD Almighty! My soul yearns, even faints, for the courts of the LORD; my heart and my flesh cry out for the living God.

Ps. 84:10. Better is one day in your courts than a thousand elsewhere; I would rather be a doorkeeper in the house of my God than dwell in the tents of the wicked.

11. **The meaning of the communion of the saints is beautifully taught in Paul's letter to Philemon.**

The Book of Philemon. *(Paul writes the letter to his "dear friend and fellow worker" on behalf of Onesimus, urging Philemon to receive him back as a "dear brother.")*

Vv. 10–12. I appeal to you for my son Onesimus, who became my son while I was in chains. Formerly he was useless to you, but now he has become useful both to you and to me. I am sending him—who is my very heart—back to you.

Vv. 15–16. Perhaps the reason he was separated from you for a little while was that you might have him back for good—no longer as a slave, but better than a slave, as a dear brother. He is very dear to me but even dearer to you, both as a man and as a brother in the Lord.

12. **Elders are God's appointed shepherds placed over the flock of Jesus Christ.**

Acts 20:28. "Keep watch over yourselves and all the flock of which the Holy Spirit has made you overseers. Be shepherds of the church of God, which he bought with his own blood."

13. Office bearers must warn the wayward.

Ezek. 33:7–9. Son of man, I have made you a watchman for the house of Israel; so hear the word I speak and give them warning from me. When I say to the wicked, "O wicked man, you will surely die," and you do not speak out to dissuade him from his ways, that wicked man will die for his sin, and I will hold you accountable for his blood. But if you do warn the wicked man to turn from his ways and he does not do so, he will die for his sin, but you will have saved yourself.

14. God condemns and warns unfaithful shepherds.

Ezek. 34:1–16.

15. Members of the church must honor and obey the elders whom God has appointed to exercise authority in the church.

1 Tim. 5:17. The elders who direct the affairs of the church well are worthy of double honor, especially those whose work is preaching and teaching.

Heb. 13:17. Obey your leaders and submit to their authority. They keep watch over you as men who must give an account. Obey them so that their work will be a joy, not a burden, for that would be of no advantage to you.

16. God's office bearers must say all and only that which he requires of them, even when they are under great pressure to do otherwise.

1 Kings 22:1–14.

1 Kings 22:8–9. The king of Israel answered Jehoshaphat (king of Judah), "There is still one man through whom we can inquire of the LORD, but I hate him because he never prophesies anything good about me, but always bad. He is Micaiah, son of Imlah." "The king should not say that," Jehoshaphat replied. So the king of Israel called one of his officials and said, "Bring Micaiah, son of Imlah at once."

1 Kings 22:13–14. The messenger who had gone to summon Micaiah said to him, "Look, as one man the other prophets are predicting success for the king. Let your word agree with theirs,

and speak favorably." But Micaiah said, "As surely as the LORD lives, I can tell him only what the LORD tells me."

17. Jesus prays for the church.

John 17:6–26. *(Jesus' high priestly prayer)*

18. The church is a great multitude gathered from all nations and tribes.

Rev. 7:9. After this I looked and there before me was a great multitude that no one could count, from every nation, tribe, people and language, standing before the throne and in front of the Lamb. They were wearing white robes and were holding palm branches in their hands.

Church Discipline

1. **Discipline begins with personal admonition.**

    Rom. 15:14. I myself am convinced, my brothers, that you your-selves are full of goodness, complete in knowledge and competent to instruct one another.

    Col. 3:16. Let the word of Christ dwell in you richly as you teach and admonish one another with all wisdom, and as you sing psalms, hymns and spiritual songs with gratitude in your hearts to God.

2. **Restore one who has fallen, with gentleness.**

    Gal. 6:1. Brothers, if someone is caught in a sin, you who are spiritual should restore him gently. But watch yourself, or you also may be tempted.

3. **Seek to save an erring sinner.**

    James 5:19–20. My brothers, if one of you should wander from the truth and someone should bring him back, remember this: Whoever turns a sinner from the error of his way will save him from death and cover over a multitude of sins.

4. **Forgive and restore one who repents; love him.**

    2 Cor. 2:7–8. Now instead, you ought to forgive and comfort him, so that he will not be overwhelmed by excessive sorrow. I urge you, therefore, to reaffirm your love for him.

5. **Do not fellowship with one who will not repent.**

    1 Cor. 5:11. Now I am writing you that you must not associate with anyone who calls himself a brother but is sexually immoral or greedy, an idolater or a slanderer, a drunkard or a swindler. With such a man do not even eat.

6. Jesus gives us the procedure for church discipline.

Matt. 18:15–18. If your brother sins against you, go and show him his fault, just between the two of you. If he listens to you, you have won your brother over. But if he will not listen, take one or two others along, so that "every matter may be established by the testimony of two or three witnesses." If he refuses to listen to them, tell it to the church; and if he refuses to listen even to the church, treat him as you would a pagan or a tax collector. I tell you the truth, whatever you bind on earth will be bound in heaven, and whatever you loose on earth will be loosed in heaven.

7. Christ has given the keys of the kingdom to the church.

Matt. 16:19. I will give you the keys of the kingdom of heaven; whatever you bind on earth will be bound in heaven, and whatever you loose on earth will be loosed in heaven.

8. Purge out the old leaven.

1 Cor. 5:1–13.

9. Excommunication is sometimes necessary.

2 Thess. 3:14. If anyone does not obey our instruction in this letter, take special note of him. Do not associate with him, in order that he may feel ashamed. Yet do not regard him as an enemy, but warn him as a brother.

10. Jesus commends the church for faithful discipline.

Rev. 2:2. I know your deeds, your hard work and your perseverance. I know that you cannot tolerate wicked men, that you have tested those who claim to be apostles but are not, and have found them false.

11. Jesus rebukes the church that does not discipline.

Rev. 2:14–16. I have a few things against you: You have people there who hold to the teaching of Balaam, who taught Balak to entice the Israelites to sin by eating food sacrificed to idols and by committing sexual immorality. Likewise you also have those who hold to the teaching of the Nicolaitans. Repent therefore! Otherwise, I will soon come to you and will fight against them with the sword of my mouth.

Comfort

See also Death, p. 51; Forgiveness of Sins, p. 72; Prayer, p. 137; Providence of God, p. 146; and Trust, p. 186.

1. **The Lord is our shepherd, always leading us in the best way and protecting us.**

   Ps. 23.

2. **As an eagle stirs up its nest and hovers over its young, so God cares for his own.**

   Deut. 32:10–12. He shielded him and cared for him; he guarded him as the apple of his eye, like an eagle that stirs up its nest and hovers over its young, that spreads its wings to catch them and carries them on its pinions. The LORD alone led him; no foreign god was with him.

3. **As a father cares for his children, so God cares for his own; his love is everlasting.**

   Ps. 103:8–18.

4. **God always shelters those who put their trust in him.**

   Ps. 91:1–2. He who dwells in the shelter of the Most High will rest in the shadow of the Almighty. I will say of the LORD, "He is my refuge and my fortress, my God, in whom I trust."

5. **God knows us most intimately; he holds and guides us by his hand.**

   Ps. 139:1–12.

Ps. 139:1–3. O LORD, you have searched me and you know me. You know when I sit and when I rise; you perceive my thoughts from afar. You discern my going out and my lying down; you are familiar with all my ways.

Ps. 139:9–10. If I rise on the wings of the dawn, if I settle on the far side of the sea, even there your hand will guide me, your right hand will hold me fast.

6. **The wicked appear to prosper for a time, while the righteous suffer; but actually God is always leading us in the best way; he comforts us with his presence.**

   Ps. 73.

   Ps. 73:23–24. I am always with you; you hold me by my right hand. You guide me with your counsel, and afterward you will take me into glory.

7. **The sufferings of the present time are not worth comparing with the coming glory.**

   Rom. 8:18. I consider that our present sufferings are not worth comparing with the glory that will be revealed in us.

8. **God works all things together for our good.**

   Rom. 8:28. We know that in all things God works for the good of those who love him, who have been called according to his purpose.

9. **If God is for us, nothing can separate us from his love.**

   Rom. 8:31–39.

   Rom. 8:31. What, then, shall we say in response to this? If God is for us, who can be against us?

   Rom. 8:38–39. I am convinced that neither death nor life, neither angels nor demons, neither the present nor the future, nor any powers, neither height nor depth, nor anything else in all creation, will be able to separate us from the love of God that is in Christ Jesus our Lord.

10. **Jesus, the good shepherd, died for his sheep; he knows, leads, and protects each one; he gives us eternal security.**

    John 10:11. I am the good shepherd. The good shepherd lays down his life for the sheep.

John 10:14–15. I am the good shepherd; I know my sheep and my sheep know me—just as the Father knows me and I know the Father—and I lay down my life for the sheep.

John 10:27–29. My sheep listen to my voice; I know them, and they follow me. I give them eternal life, and they shall never perish; no one can snatch them out of my hand. My Father, who has given them to me, is greater than all; no one can snatch them out of my Father's hand.

11. **God's grace is sufficient for every need.**

     2 Cor. 9:8. God is able to make all grace abound to you, so that in all things at all times, having all that you need, you will abound in every good work.

12. **Paul had a thorn in the flesh; God's promise: My grace is sufficient for you.**

     2 Cor. 12:7–10.

     2 Cor. 12:9. He said to me, "My grace is sufficient for you, for my power is made perfect in weakness." Therefore I will boast all the more gladly about my weaknesses, so that Christ's power may rest on me.

13. **Jesus rebuked the disciples for their little faith and calmed the storm.**

     Matt. 8:23–27.

14. **God directs all things by his infinite wisdom and his ways are beyond tracing out.**

     Rom. 11:33–36. Oh, the depth of the riches of the wisdom and knowledge of God! How unsearchable his judgments, and his paths beyond tracing out! "Who has known the mind of the Lord? Or who has been his counselor?" "Who has ever given to God, that God should repay him?" For from him and through him and to him are all things. To him be the glory forever! Amen.

15. **One day this life of suffering will be over and all will be made new.**

     Rev. 21:1–4.

     Rev. 21:3–4. I heard a loud voice from the throne saying, "Now the dwelling of God is with men, and he will live with them. They will be his people, and God himself will be with them and be their

God. He will wipe every tear from their eyes. There will be no more death or mourning or crying or pain, for the old order of things has passed away."

16. Cast your concerns on the Lord, for he will support you.

Ps. 55:22. Cast your cares on the LORD and he will sustain you; he will never let the righteous fall.

17. God is the source of all comfort.

2 Cor. 1:3–4. Praise be to the God and Father of our Lord Jesus Christ, the Father of compassion and the God of all comfort, who comforts us in all our troubles, so that we can comfort those in any trouble with the comfort we ourselves have received from God.

18. God is unchangeably faithful.

Ps. 89:1–8.

Ps. 89:1–2. I will sing of the LORD's great love forever; with my mouth I will make your faithfulness known through all generations. I will declare that your love stands firm forever, that you established your faithfulness in heaven itself.

Ps. 89:8. O LORD God Almighty, who is like you? You are mighty, O LORD, and your faithfulness surrounds you.

19. The Lord tends his flock like a shepherd.

Isa. 40:10–11. See, the Sovereign LORD comes with power, and his arm rules for him. See, his reward is with him, and his recompense accompanies him. He tends his flock like a shepherd: He gathers the lambs in his arms and he carries them close to his heart; he gently leads those that have young.

20. God's favor lasts for a lifetime. He turns weeping into rejoicing.

Ps. 30:4–5. Sing to the LORD, you saints of his; praise his holy name. For his anger lasts only a moment, but his favor lasts a lifetime; weeping may remain for a night, but rejoicing comes in the morning.

21. God has made a commitment to supply all your actual needs.

Phil. 4:19. And my God will meet all your needs according to his glorious riches in Christ Jesus.

Communication, Gossip, Lying

1. The psalmist has given us a model prayer for good speech.

Ps. 19:14. May the words of my mouth and the meditation of my heart be pleasing in your sight, O LORD, my Rock and my Redeemer.

Ps. 141:3. Set a guard over my mouth, O LORD; keep watch over the door of my lips.

2. Commit yourself to speaking only what is right and true.

Prov. 8:6–8. Listen, for I have worthy things to say; I open my lips to speak what is right. My mouth speaks what is true, for my lips detest wickedness. All the words of my mouth are just; none of them is crooked or perverse.

3. Speak the truth in love, not harshly.

Eph. 4:15. Instead, speaking the truth in love, we will in all things grow up into him who is the Head, that is, Christ.

Eph. 4:29. Do not let any unwholesome talk come out of your mouths, but only what is helpful for building others up according to their needs, that it may benefit those who listen.

4. Avoid harsh words.

Prov. 15:1. A gentle answer turns away wrath, but a harsh word stirs up anger.

5. Be quick to listen, slow to speak.

James 1:19. My dear brothers, take note of this: Everyone should be quick to listen, slow to speak and slow to become angry.

Eccles. 5:3–5. As a dream comes when there are many cares, so the speech of a fool when there are many words. When you make a vow to God, do not delay in fulfilling it. He has no pleasure in fools; fulfill your vow. It is better not to vow than to make a vow and not fulfill it.

Prov. 10:19. When words are many, sin is not absent, but he who holds his tongue is wise.

Prov. 15:28. The heart of the righteous weighs its answers, but the mouth of the wicked gushes evil.

Prov. 17:28. Even a fool is thought wise if he keeps silent, and discerning if he holds his tongue.

6. **Listen before you speak.**

Prov. 18:13. He who answers before listening—that is his folly and his shame.

Prov. 29:20. Do you see a man who speaks in haste? There is more hope for a fool than for him.

7. **God forbids us to lie; he wants us to speak the truth.**

Exod. 20:16. You shall not give false testimony against your neighbor.

Eph. 4:25. Each of you must put off falsehood and speak truthfully to his neighbor, for we are all members of one body.

8. **The Lord detests lying.**

Prov. 12:22. The LORD detests lying lips, but he delights in men who are truthful.

Ps. 34:11–14. Come, my children, listen to me; I will teach you the fear of the LORD. Whoever of you loves life and desires to see many good days, keep your tongue from evil and your lips from speaking lies. Turn from evil and do good; seek peace and pursue it.

9. **All lying is of the devil, the father of all lies.**

John 8:44. There is no truth in him [the devil]. When he lies, he speaks his native language, for he is a liar and the father of lies.

10. **Lying will be punished.**

Prov. 19:9. A false witness will not go unpunished, and he who pours out lies will perish.

11. **Do not hurt your neighbor by gossip or careless talk; control your tongue.**

   Prov. 11:11–13. Through the blessing of the upright a city is exalted, but by the mouth of the wicked it is destroyed. A man who lacks judgment derides his neighbor, but a man of understanding holds his tongue. A gossip betrays a confidence, but a trustworthy man keeps a secret.

   Prov. 12:18. Reckless words pierce like a sword, but the tongue of the wise brings healing.

   Prov. 17:27–28. A man of knowledge uses words with restraint, and a man of understanding is even-tempered. Even a fool is thought wise if he keeps silent, and discerning if he holds his tongue.

   Prov. 29:19. A gossip betrays a confidence; so avoid a man who talks too much.

   Prov. 21:23. He who guards his mouth and his tongue keeps himself from calamity.

12. **Tame the tongue; it can be very destructive.**

   James 3:1–12.

13. **We must help stop gossip and strife.**

   Prov. 26:20. Without wood a fire goes out; without gossip a quarrel dies down.

14. **Be careful. Don't speak rashly.**

   Prov. 13:3. He who guards his lips guards his soul, but he who speaks rashly will come to ruin.

15. **A word aptly spoken and a wise rebuke can be very helpful to others.**

   Prov. 25:11–12. A word aptly spoken is like apples of gold in settings of silver. Like an earring of gold or an ornament of fine gold is a wise man's rebuke to a listening ear.

   Prov. 15:4. The tongue that brings healing is a tree of life, but a deceitful tongue crushes the spirit.

Conscience

1. **Keep a clear conscience.**

   1 Peter 3:15–16. In your hearts set apart Christ as Lord. Always be prepared to give an answer to everyone who asks you to give the reason for the hope that you have. But do this with gentleness and respect, keeping a clear conscience, so that those who speak maliciously against your good behavior in Christ may be ashamed of their slander.

2. **Keep a clear conscience before God and men.**

   Acts 24:16. I strive always to keep my conscience clear before God and man.

3. **Hold to the truths of the faith.**

   1 Tim. 3:9. They [deacons] must keep hold of the deep truths of the faith with a clear conscience.

4. **A conscience can be seared.**

   1 Tim. 4:2. Such teachings come through hypocritical liars, whose consciences have been seared as with a hot iron.

5. **You can have a clear conscience and rest in the heart.**

   Prov. 3:21–26. My son, preserve sound judgment and discernment, do not let them out of your sight; they will be life for you, an ornament to grace your neck. Then you will go on your way in safety, and your foot will not stumble; when you lie down, you will not be afraid; when you lie down, your sleep will be sweet.

6. **Christ will give you a clear conscience.**

   Heb. 9:14. How much more, then, will the blood of Christ, who through the eternal Spirit offered himself unblemished to God, cleanse our consciences from acts that lead to death, so that we may serve the living God.

7. A guilty conscience can be cleansed.

Heb. 10:22. Let us draw near to God with a sincere heart in full assurance of faith, having our hearts sprinkled to cleanse us from a guilty conscience and having our bodies washed with pure water.

Contentment, Coveting, Priorities

Note: To be content is to accept in faith, with a thankful heart and submissive spirit, that which God in his grace and wisdom ordains for us.

1. **Godliness with contentment is great gain.**

   1 Tim. 6:6. Godliness with contentment is great gain.

2. **Learn contentment, for love of money brings misery.**

   1 Tim. 6:7–10. We brought nothing into the world, and we can take nothing out of it. But if we have food and clothing, we will be content with that. People who want to get rich fall into temptation and a trap and into many foolish and harmful desires that plunge men into ruin and destruction. For the love of money is a root of all kinds of evil. Some people, eager for money, have wandered from the faith and pierced themselves with many griefs.

3. **Keep free from love of money and be content.**

   Heb. 13:5. Keep your lives free from the love of money and be content with what you have, because God has said, "Never will I leave you; never will I forsake you" [Deut. 31:6].

4. **Paul learned contentment even in the most difficult circumstances of life.**

   Phil. 4:11–13. I am not saying this because I am in need, for I have learned to be content whatever the circumstances. I know what it is to be in need, and I know what it is to have plenty. I have learned the secret of being content in any and every situation, whether well fed or hungry, whether living in plenty or in want. I can do everything through him who gives me strength.

5. Contentment promotes peace.

Prov. 17:1. Better a dry crust with peace and quiet than a house full of feasting, with strife.

6. Life does not consist of what one possesses.

Luke 12:15. Then he [Jesus] said to them, "Watch out! Be on your guard against all kinds of greed; a man's life does not consist in the abundance of his possessions."

7. The parable of the rich fool teaches that life is more than material riches.

Luke 12:16–21. *(The rich fool stored up things for himself but was not rich toward God, so his life was demanded of him.)*

8. Do not allow the deceitfulness of wealth to crowd out the word.

Mark 4:1–20. *(the parable of the sower)*

Mark 4:7, 18–20. Other seed fell among thorns, which grew up and choked the plants, so that they did not bear grain. . . . [Other people], like seed among thorns, hear the word; but the worries of this life, the deceitfulness of wealth and the desires for other things come in and choke the word, making it unfruitful.

9. Put covetousness to death.

Col. 3:5. Put to death, therefore, whatever belongs to your earthly nature: sexual immorality, impurity, lust, evil desires and greed, which is idolatry.

10. Do not lay up earthly treasures, but heavenly treasures.

Matt. 6:19–21. Do not store up for yourselves treasures on earth, where moth and rust destroy, and where thieves break in and steal. But store up for yourselves treasures in heaven, where moth and rust do not destroy, and where thieves do not break in and steal. For where your treasure is, there your heart will be also.

11. You can't serve two masters at one time.

Matt. 6:24. No one can serve two masters. Either he will hate the one and love the other, or he will be devoted to the one and despise the other. You cannot serve both God and Money.

12. Seek first God's kingdom.

Matt. 6:33. Seek first his kingdom and his righteousness, and all these things will be given to you as well.

13. Don't seek status, as the disciples did.

Luke 9:46–48. An argument started among the disciples as to which of them would be the greatest. Jesus, knowing their thoughts, took a little child and had him stand beside him. Then he said to them, "Whoever welcomes this little child in my name welcomes me; and whoever welcomes me welcomes the one who sent me. For he who is least among you all—he is the greatest."

14. It's better to have a simple lifestyle than to have wealth with a lot of conflict in the home.

Prov. 15:16–17. Better a little with the fear of the LORD than great wealth with turmoil. Better a meal of vegetables where there is love than a fattened calf with hatred.

Prov. 17:1. Better a dry crust with peace and quiet than a house full of feasting with strife.

15. Don't wear yourself out to get rich.

Prov. 23:4–5. Do not wear yourself out to get rich; have the wisdom to show restraint. Cast but a glance at riches, and they are gone, for they will surely sprout wings and fly off to the sky like an eagle.

Prov. 28:6. Better a poor man whose walk is blameless than a rich man whose ways are perverse.

Eccles. 4:6. Better one handful with tranquillity than two handfuls with toil and chasing after the wind.

16. Seek neither poverty nor riches.

Prov. 30:8–9. Keep falsehood and lies far from me; give me neither poverty nor riches, but give me only my daily bread. Otherwise, I may have too much and disown you and say, "Who is the LORD?" Or I may become poor and steal, and so dishonor the name of my God.

17. It's better to have wisdom than to have wealth.

Prov. 16:16–17. How much better to get wisdom than gold, to choose understanding rather than silver! The highway of the upright avoids evil; he who guards his way guards his soul.

18. A good name is more desirable than great riches.

Prov. 22:1. A good name is more desirable than great riches; to be esteemed is better than silver or gold.

19. King Ahab's unchecked covetousness finally drove him to murder.
1 Kings 21:1–14.

1 Kings 21:2–4. Ahab said to Naboth, "Let me have your vineyard to use for a vegetable garden, since it is close to my palace. In exchange I will give you a better vineyard or, if you prefer, I will pay you whatever it is worth." But Naboth replied, "The LORD forbid that I should give you the inheritance of my fathers." So Ahab went home, sullen and angry because Naboth the Jezreelite had said, "I will not give you the inheritance of my fathers." He lay on his bed sulking and refused to eat.

20. **King Hezekiah had his priorities turned around. In pride he displayed earthly riches, and was judged for it.**

    2 Kings 20:12–19.

    2 Kings 20:14–19. Then Isaiah the prophet went to King Hezekiah and asked, "What did those men say, and where did they come from?" "From a distant land," Hezekiah replied. "They came from Babylon." The prophet asked, "What did they see in your palace?" "They saw everything in my palace," Hezekiah said. "There is nothing among my treasures that I did not show them." Then Isaiah said to Hezekiah, "Hear the word of the LORD: The time will surely come when everything in your palace, and all that your fathers have stored up until this day, will be carried off to Babylon. Nothing will be left, says the LORD. And some of your descendants, your own flesh and blood, that will be born to you, will be taken away, and they will become eunuchs in the palace of the king of Babylon." "The word of the LORD you have spoken is good," Hezekiah replied. For he thought, "Will there not be peace and security in my lifetime?"

21. **Habakkuk was content with God's way and trusted him even when things looked very hard.**

    Hab. 3:17–19. Though the fig tree does not bud and there are no grapes on the vines, though the olive crop fails and the fields produce no food, though there are no sheep in the pen and no cattle in the stalls, yet I will rejoice in the LORD, I will be joyful in God my Savior. The Sovereign LORD is my strength; he makes my feet like the feet of a deer, he enables me to go on the heights.

22. **God chastised Gehazi severely for his covetousness.**

    2 Kings 5:19–27. *(Gehazi deceitfully obtains a gift from Naaman.)*

    2 Kings 5:19–20. After Naaman had traveled some distance, Gehazi, the servant of Elisha the man of God, said to himself, "My master was too easy on Naaman, this Aramean, by not accepting

from him what he brought. As surely as the LORD lives, I will run after him and get something from him."

2 Kings 5:27. "Naaman's leprosy will cling to you and to your descendants forever." Then Gehazi went from Elisha's presence and he was leprous, as white as snow.

23. Riches are meaningless; wealth is fleeting.

Eccles. 5:8–17.

Eccles. 5:10–11. Whoever loves money never has money enough; whoever loves wealth is never satisfied with his income. This too is meaningless. As goods increase, so those who consume them. And what benefit are they to the owner, except to feast his eyes on?

Eccles. 5:15–17. Naked a man comes from his mother's womb, and as he comes, so he departs. He takes nothing from his labor that he can carry on his hand. This too is a grievous evil: as a man comes, so he departs, and what does he gain, since he toils for the wind? All his days he eats in darkness, with great frustration, affliction and anger.

24. The primary goal in life must be to fear God and keep his commandments.

Eccles. 12:13–14. Now all has been heard; here is the conclusion of the matter: Fear God and keep his commandments, for this is the whole duty of man. For God will bring every deed into judgment, including every hidden thing, whether it is good or evil.

Matt. 6:33. But seek first his kingdom and his righteousness, and all these things will be given to you as well.

25. What is seen is temporary, but what is unseen is eternal.

2 Cor. 4:18. So we fix our eyes not on what is seen, but on what is unseen. For what is seen is temporary, but what is unseen is eternal.

26. Set your affections on the things above, not on things on the earth.

Col. 3:1–3. Since, then, you have been raised with Christ, set your hearts on things above, where Christ is seated at the right hand of God. Set your minds on things above, not on earthly things. For you died, and your life is now hidden with Christ in God.

27. The righteous will be ready to give liberally, rather than to be covetous.

Prov. 21:6. All day long he [the sluggard] craves for more, but the righteous give without sparing.

Death, Eternal Life

In the case of the death of a child, see also Children, p. 28.

1. You can face death without fear.

Ps. 23:4. Even though I walk through the valley of the shadow of death, I will fear no evil, for you are with me; your rod and your staff, they comfort me.

2. The believer will dwell in God's house forever.

Ps. 23:6. Surely goodness and love will follow me all the days of my life, and I will dwell in the house of the LORD forever.

John 14:1–4. "Do not let your hearts be troubled. Trust in God; trust also in me. In my Father's house are many rooms; if it were not so, I would have told you. I am going to prepare a place for you. And if I go and prepare a place for you, I will come back and take you to be with me that you also may be where I am. You know the way to the place where I am going."

3. To live is Christ; to die is gain.

Phil. 1:21. For to me, to live is Christ and to die is gain.

4. Paul wanted both to remain here, and to go home to be with the Lord, which is far better.

Phil. 1:22–26.

Phil. 1:23–24. I am torn between the two: I desire to depart and be with Christ, which is better by far; but it is more necessary for you that I remain in the body.

5. The death of the Lord's saints is precious.

Ps. 116:15. Precious in the sight of the LORD is the death of his saints.

6. **Those who die in the Lord are blessed.**

   Rev. 14:13. Then I heard a voice from heaven say, "Write: Blessed are the dead who die in the Lord from now on." "Yes," says the Spirit, "they will rest from their labor, for their deeds will follow them."

7. **You can have comfort concerning those who have died and are asleep in Jesus.**

   1 Thess. 4:13–18.

   1 Thess. 4:16–18. For the Lord himself will come down from heaven, with a loud command, with the voice of the archangel and with the trumpet call of God, and the dead in Christ will rise first. After that, we who are still alive and are left will be caught up together with them in the clouds to meet the Lord in the air. And so we will be with the Lord forever. Therefore encourage each other with these words.

8. **Believers who have died are absent from the body, but at home with the Lord.**

   2 Cor. 5:1–8. *(our heavenly dwellings)*

   2 Cor. 5:6–8. We are always confident and know that as long as we are at home in the body we are away from the Lord. We live by faith, not by sight. We are confident, I say, and would prefer to be away from the body and at home with the Lord.

9. **In life and death we are the Lord's.**

   Rom. 14:8. If we live, we live to the Lord; and if we die, we die to the Lord. So, whether we live or die, we belong to the Lord.

10. **Jesus comforted Mary and Martha after Lazarus died. He is the resurrection and the life.**

    John 11:17–26.

    John 11:23–26. Jesus said to her [Martha], "Your brother will rise again." Martha answered, "I know he will rise again in the resurrection at the last day." Jesus said to her, "I am the resurrection and the life. He who believes in me will live, even though he dies; and whoever lives and believes in me will never die. Do you believe this?"

11. **The perishable will put on the imperishable; death will be swallowed up in victory.**

    1 Cor. 15:54–57. Then the saying that is written will come true: "Death has been swallowed up in victory." "Where, O death, is

your victory? Where, O death, is your sting?" The sting of death is sin, and the power of sin is the law. But thanks be to God! He gives us the victory through our Lord Jesus Christ.

12. Believers are co-heirs with Christ.

Rom. 8:16–17. The Spirit himself testifies with our spirit that we are God's children. Now if we are children, then we are heirs— heirs of God and co-heirs with Christ, if indeed we share in his sufferings in order that we may also share in his glory.

13. Nothing—not even death—can separate us from the love of God.
Rom. 8:35–39.

Rom. 8:38–39. I am convinced that neither death nor life, neither angels nor demons, neither the present nor the future, nor any powers, neither height nor depth, nor anything else in all creation, will be able to separate us from the love of God that is in Christ Jesus our Lord.

14. When David's infant son died, he was comforted by the knowledge that one day he would go to him.

2 Sam. 12:18–23.

2 Sam. 12:23. Now that he is dead, why should I fast? Can I bring him back again? I will go to him, but he will not return to me.

15. Jesus, the good shepherd, laid down his life for his sheep.

John 10:14–15. I am the good shepherd; I know my sheep and my sheep know me—just as the Father knows me and I know the Father—and I lay down my life for the sheep.

16. Jesus' sheep hear his voice and follow him, and he gives them eternal life. No one can snatch them out of his hand.

John 10:27–30. My sheep listen to my voice; I know them, and they follow me. I give them eternal life, and they shall never perish; no one can snatch them out of my hand. My Father, who has given them to me, is greater than all; no one can snatch them out of my Father's hand. I and the Father are one.

17. There will be a new heaven and a new earth in which there will be no more suffering or sorrowing.

Rev. 21:1–4. Then I saw a new heaven and a new earth, for the first heaven and the first earth had passed away, and there was no longer any sea. I saw the Holy City, the new Jerusalem, coming down out of heaven from God, prepared as a bride beautifully dressed for her husband. And I heard a loud voice from the throne, saying, "Now the dwelling of God is with men, and he will live with them. They will be his people, and God himself will be with them and be their God. He will wipe every tear from their eyes. There will be no more death or mourning or crying or pain, for the old order of things has passed away."

18. Jesus died so that we may live forever with him. Encourage one another with this truth.

1 Thess. 5:9–11. God did not appoint us to suffer wrath but to receive salvation through our Lord Jesus Christ. He died for us so that, whether we are awake or asleep, we may live together with him. Therefore encourage one another and build each other up, just as in fact you are doing.

19. All who believe in Jesus will have eternal life.

John 3:14–15. Just as Moses lifted up the snake in the desert, so the Son of Man must be lifted up, that everyone who believes in him may have eternal life.

John 3:16. God so loved the world that he gave his one and only Son, that whoever believes in him shall not perish but have eternal life.

John 3:36. Whoever believes in the Son has eternal life, but whoever rejects the Son will not see life, for God's wrath remains on him.

1 John 5:11–12. This is the testimony: God has given us eternal life, and this life is in his Son. He who has the Son has life; he who does not have the Son of God does not have life.

20. When Jesus comes again, he will separate the sheep from the goats.

Matt. 25:31–46.

Matt. 25:31–34. When the Son of Man comes in his glory, and all the angels with him, he will sit on his throne in heavenly glory. All the nations will be gathered before him, and he will separate the people one from another as a shepherd separates the sheep from the goats. He will put the sheep on his right and the goats on his left. Then the King will say to those on his right, "Come, you who are blessed by my Father; take your inheritance, the kingdom prepared for you since the creation of the world."

Matt. 25:41. Then he will say to those on his left, "Depart from me, you who are cursed, into the eternal fire prepared for the devil and his angels."

Matt. 25:46. Then they will go away to eternal punishment, but the righteous to eternal life.

21. After Jesus comes again believers will be like him.

1 John 3:1–2. How great is the love the father has lavished on us, that we should be called children of God! And that is what we are! The reason the world does not know us is that it did not know him. Dear friends, now we are children of God, and what we will be has not yet been made known. But we know that when he appears, we shall be like him, for we shall see him as he is.

22. Everyone who has this hope (certainty) will strive to live a pure life.

1 John 3:3. Everyone who has this hope in him purifies himself, just as he is pure.

23. Christians are guaranteed an inheritance that can never be destroyed.

1 Peter 1:3–9.

1 Peter 1:3–5. Praise be to the God and Father of our Lord Jesus Christ! In his great mercy he has given us new birth into a living hope through the resurrection of Jesus Christ from the dead, and into an inheritance that can never perish, spoil or fade—kept in heaven for you, who through faith are shielded by God's power until the coming of the salvation that is ready to be revealed in the last time.

24. Every Christian who has fought the good fight of faith will, like Paul, receive the crown of righteousness.

2 Tim. 4:7–8. I have fought the good fight, I have finished the race, I have kept the faith. Now there is in store for me the crown of righteousness, which the Lord, the righteous judge, will award me on that day—and not only to me, but also to all who have longed for his appearing.

25. **With our spiritual father, Abraham, we can, as pilgrims, look forward to the city with foundations, whose architect and builder is God.**

    Heb. 11:9–10. By faith he [Abraham] made his home in the promised land like a stranger in a foreign country; he lived in tents, as did Isaac and Jacob, who were heirs with him of the same promise. For he was looking forward to the city with foundations, whose architect and builder is God.

26. **Our citizenship is in heaven. There our bodies will be like the glorious body of Jesus Christ.**

    Phil. 3:20–21. But our citizenship is in heaven. And we eagerly await a Savior from there, the Lord Jesus Christ, who, by the power that enables him to bring everything under his control, will transform our lowly bodies so that they will be like his glorious body.

27. **Jesus' resurrection guarantees ours.**

    1 Cor. 15:12–23.

    1 Cor. 15:20–23. But Christ has indeed been raised from the dead, the firstfruits of those who have fallen asleep. For since death came through a man, the resurrection of the dead comes also through a man. For as in Adam all die, so in Christ all will be made alive. But each in his own turn: Christ, the firstfruits; then, when he comes, those who belong to him.

28. **Paul describes the beauty and glory of our imperishable, incorruptible resurrection bodies and declares that death will be swallowed up in victory.**

    1 Cor. 15:35–57.

29. **Jesus gives wonderful promises to all who overcome, who conquer, who fight against sin and in their love for Christ persevere.**

    Rev. 2:11. He who overcomes will not be hurt at all by the second death.

    Rev. 2:26–28. To him who overcomes and does my will to the end, I will give authority over the nations—"He will rule them with an iron scepter; he will dash them to pieces like pottery"—just as I have received authority from my Father. I will also give him the morning star. He who has an ear, let him hear what the Spirit says to the churches.

Rev. 3:4–5. Yet you have a few people in Sardis who have not soiled their clothes. They will walk with me, dressed in white, for they are worthy. He who overcomes will, like them, be dressed in white. I will never blot out his name from the book of life, but will acknowledge his name before my Father and his angels.

Rev. 3:12. Him who overcomes I will make like a pillar in the temple of my God.

Rev. 3:21–22. To him who overcomes, I will give the right to sit with me on my throne, just as I overcame and sat down with my Father on his throne. He who has an ear, let him hear what the Spirit says to the churches.

Decision Making

1. Joshua called the Israelites to make a decision.

Josh. 24:14–27.

Josh. 24:14–15. Now fear the LORD and serve him with all faithfulness. Throw away the gods your forefathers worshiped beyond the River and in Egypt, and serve the LORD. But if serving the LORD seems undesirable to you, then choose for yourselves this day whom you will serve. . . . But as for me and my household, we will serve the LORD.

2. God's people make a covenantal commitment.

Josh. 24:19–27.

Josh. 24:24–25. And the people said to Joshua, "We will serve the LORD our God and obey him."

3. Elijah called God's people to stop wavering.

1 Kings 18:16–39.

1 Kings 18:21. How long will you waver between two opinions? If the LORD is God, follow him; but if Baal is God, follow him.

4. Today, if you hear his voice, don't harden your hearts (a warning against unbelief and rebellion).

Heb. 3:7–11. As the Holy Spirit says: "Today, if you hear his voice, do not harden your hearts as you did in the rebellion, during the time of testing in the desert, where your fathers tested and tried me and for forty years saw what I did. That is why I was angry with that generation, and I said, 'Their hearts are always going astray, and they have not known my ways.' So I declared on oath in my anger, 'They shall never enter my rest.'"

5. Moses' decision is a good example to follow.

Heb. 11:24–26. By faith Moses, when he had grown up, refused to be known as the son of Pharaoh's daughter. He chose to be mistreated along with the people of God rather than to enjoy the pleasures of sin for a short time.

6. Make a full commitment.

Rom. 12:1–2. I urge you, brothers, in view of God's mercy, to offer your bodies as living sacrifices, holy and pleasing to God—which is your spiritual worship. Do not conform any longer to the pattern of this world, but be transformed by the renewing of your mind. Then you will be able to test and approve what God's will is—his good, pleasing and perfect will.

Depression

See also Comfort, p. 37; Prayer, p. 137; Providence of God, p. 146; and Trust, p. 186.

1. **Concealing sin often leads to depression. If you confess your sins and turn from them you will find mercy.**

   Prov. 28:13. He who conceals his sins does not prosper, but whoever confesses and renounces them finds mercy.

2. **Cain's depression was due to guilt.**

   Gen. 4:6–7. Then the LORD said to Cain, "Why are you angry? Why is your face downcast? If you do what is right, will you not be accepted? But if you do not do what is right, sin is crouching at your door; it desires to have you, but you must master it."

3. **David was very depressed until he confessed his sin of adultery.**

   Ps. 32:3–4. When I kept silent, my bones wasted away through my groaning all day long. For day and night your hand was heavy upon me; my strength was sapped as in the heat of summer.

4. **The way out of depression caused by guilt is confession and seeking God's forgiveness.**

   Ps. 32:5. Then I acknowledged my sin to you and did not cover up my iniquity. I said, "I will confess my transgressions to the LORD"—and you forgave the guilt of my sin.

   Ps. 32:1–2, 11 [Then David could sing for joy again]. Blessed is he whose transgressions are forgiven, whose sins are covered. Blessed is the man whose sin the LORD does not count against him and in whose spirit is no deceit. . . . Rejoice in the LORD and be glad, you righteous; sing all you who are upright in heart!

5. **Put your hope in God when you are downcast.**

    Ps. 42.

    Ps. 42:5–6. Why are you downcast, O my soul? Why so disturbed within me? Put your hope in God, for I will yet praise him, my Savior and my God.

6. **Words of comfort were given to the faithful of Israel as they became depressed while in Babylon. They were called to put their faith into action in their dark hour.**

    Isa. 40.

7. **We may experience some tough situations, but we can avoid deep depression.**

    2 Cor. 4:8–9. We are hard pressed on every side, but not crushed; perplexed, but not in despair; persecuted, but not abandoned; struck down, but not destroyed.

    2 Cor. 4:16–18. We do not lose heart. Though outwardly we are wasting away, yet inwardly we are being renewed day by day. For our light and momentary troubles are achieving for us an internal glory that far outweighs them all. So we fix our eyes not on what is seen, but on what is unseen. For what is seen is temporary, but what is unseen is eternal.

8. **Think of what Paul went through, without getting depressed, sustained by God's grace.**

    2 Cor. 11:23–28. I have worked much harder, been in prison more frequently, been flogged more severely, and been exposed to death again and again. Five times I received from the Jews the forty lashes minus one. Three times I was beaten with rods, once I was stoned, three times I was shipwrecked, I spent a night and a day in the open sea, I have been constantly on the move. I have been in danger from rivers, in danger from bandits, in danger from my own country-men, in danger from Gentiles; in danger in the city, in danger in the country, in danger at sea; and in danger from false brothers. I have labored and toiled and have often gone without sleep; I have known hunger and thirst and have often gone without food; I have been cold and naked. Besides everything else, I face daily the pressure of my concern for all the churches.

Divorce

See also Marriage, Husband/Wife Relationships, p. 105.

1. **When God instituted marriage he made it clear that the marriage bond is to be permanent.**

    Gen. 2:24. For this reason a man will leave his father and mother and be united to his wife, and they will become one flesh.

2. **God rebuked the Israelites for the sin of divorce and commanded them to be faithful to their covenant vows.**

    Mal. 2:13–16.

3. **God hates divorce.**

    Mal. 2:16. "I hate divorce," says the LORD God of Israel, "and I hate a man's covering himself with violence as well as with his garment," says the LORD Almighty. So guard yourself in your spirit, and do not break faith.

4. **Jesus says: No divorce, except in the case of adultery.**

    Matt. 5:31–32. It has been said, "Anyone who divorces his wife must give her a certificate of divorce." But I tell you that anyone who divorces his wife, except for marital unfaithfulness, causes her to commit adultery, and anyone who marries a woman so divorced commits adultery.

    Matt. 19:3–9.

    Matt. 19:4–6. "Haven't you read," he replied, "that at the beginning the Creator 'made them male and female,' and said, 'For this reason a man will leave his father and mother and be united to his wife, and the two will become one flesh'? So they are no longer two, but one. Therefore what God has joined together, let man not separate."

5. **Husband and wife are bound together until death separates them.**

Rom. 7:1–3. Do you not know, brothers—for I am speaking to men who know the law—that the law has authority over a man only as long as he lives? For example, by law a married woman is bound to her husband as long as he is alive, but if her husband dies, she is released from the law of marriage. So then, if she marries another man while her husband is still alive, she is called an adulteress. But if her husband dies, she is released from that law and is not an adulteress, even though she marries another man.

6. **Mosaic law speaks of a bill of divorcement.**
Deut. 24:1–4.

7. **A believer may not initiate a divorce from an unbelieving spouse.**
1 Cor. 7:10–16.

8. **If the unbelieving spouse wants to depart, he or she may do so.**

1 Cor. 7:15. If the unbeliever leaves, let him do so. A believing man or woman is not bound in such circumstances.

9. **The believing spouse must seek reconciliation when trouble arises.**

Rom. 12:18. If it is possible, as far as it depends on you, live at peace with everyone.

Matt. 5:23–24. If you are offering your gift at the altar and there remember that your brother has something against you, leave your gift there in front of the altar. First go and be reconciled to your brother; then come and offer your gift.

Matt. 18:15–18. If your brother sins against you, go and show him his fault, just between the two of you. If he listens to you, you have won your brother over. But if he will not listen, take one or two others along, so that "every matter may be established by the testimony of two or three witnesses." If he refuses to listen to them, tell it to the church; and if he refuses to listen even to the church, treat him as you would a pagan or a tax collector.

Example
(Good or Bad)

1. **Be a godly example for others to follow.**

    1 Tim. 4:12. Don't let anyone look down on you because you are young, but set an example for the believers in speech, in life, in love, in faith and in purity.

2. **Pastors and elders are to be good examples for the flock.**

    1 Peter 5:2–4. Be shepherds of God's flock that is under your care, serving as overseers—not because you must, but because you are willing, as God wants you to be; not greedy for money, but eager to serve; not lording it over those entrusted to you, but being examples to the flock. And when the Chief Shepherd appears, you will receive the crown of glory that will never fade away.

3. **The apostle Paul set a godly example to teach others how a Christian ought to live.**

    1 Cor. 4:15–16. In Christ Jesus I became your father through the gospel. Therefore I urge you to imitate me.

    1 Cor. 11:1. Follow my example, as I follow the example of Christ.

    2 Thess. 3:7–8. You yourselves know how you ought to follow our example. We were not idle when we were with you, nor did we eat anyone's food without paying for it. On the contrary, we worked night and day, laboring and toiling so that we would not be a burden to any of you.

4. **Paul taught new Christians at Thessalonica by his godly example and so they soon became good examples for others.**

    1 Thess. 1:5–7. You know how we lived among you for your sake. You became imitators of us and of the Lord. . . . And so you became a model to all the believers in Macedonia and Achaia.

5. **Jesus warns us never to set a bad example and cause others to sin.**

   Matt. 5:19. Anyone who breaks one of the least of these commandments and teaches others to do the same will be called least in the kingdom of heaven, but whoever practices and teaches these commands will be called great in the kingdom of heaven.

   Matt. 18:6. If anyone causes one of these little ones who believe in me to sin, it would be better for him to have a large millstone hung around his neck and to be drowned in the depths of the sea.

   Luke 17:1–3. Jesus said to his disciples, "Things that cause people to sin are bound to come, but woe to that person through whom they come. It would be better for him to be thrown into the sea with a millstone tied around his neck than for him to cause one of these little ones to sin. So watch yourselves."

6. **Don't ever put a stumbling block in another person's way.**

   Rom. 14:13. Let us stop passing judgment on one another. Instead, make up your mind not to put any stumbling block or obstacle in your brother's way.

7. **One must be ready to give up that which is in itself indifferent rather than to cause another to sin.**

   Rom. 14:1–21.

   Rom. 14:19–21. Let us therefore make every effort to do what leads to peace and to mutual edification. Do not destroy the work of God for the sake of food. All food is clean, but it is wrong for a man to eat anything that causes someone else to stumble. It is better not to eat meat or drink wine or to do anything else that will cause your brother to fall.

   1 Cor. 8:1–13. *(Paul deals with the matter of eating food sacrificed to idols.)*

   1 Cor. 8:9–13. Be careful, however, that the exercise of your freedom does not become a stumbling block to the weak. For if anyone with a weak conscience sees you who have this knowledge eating in an idol's temple, won't he be emboldened to eat what has been sacrificed to idols? So this weak brother, for whom Christ died, is destroyed by your knowledge. When you sin against your brothers in this way and wound their weak conscience, you sin against Christ. Therefore, if what I eat causes my brother to fall into sin, I will never eat meat again, so that I will not cause him to fall.

False Prophets, Teachers

Note: False prophets and false teachers arise from within the church. They always put on a false front and often mix truth with error. They are, therefore, often difficult to detect. This requires watchfulness.

1. **False prophets promise peace when there is no peace. They tell you that you can live in sin and God will not punish you.**

    Jer. 14:11–16.

    Jer. 14:13–14. I said, "Ah, Sovereign LORD, the prophets keep telling them 'You will not see the sword or suffer famine. Indeed, I will give you lasting peace in this place.'" Then the Lord said to me, "The prophets are prophesying lies in my name. I have not sent them or appointed them or spoken to them. They are prophesying to you false visions, divinations, idolatries and the delusions of their own minds."

2. **God reveals the terrible damage false prophets do in the church and warns against them.**

    Jer. 23:1–40.

3. **God warns against the false shepherds who destroy and scatter the flock.**

    Jer. 23:1–4. "Woe to the shepherds who are destroying and scattering the sheep of my pasture!" declares the LORD. Therefore this is what the LORD, the God of Israel, says to the shepherds who tend my people: "Because you have scattered my flock and driven them away and have not bestowed care on them, I will bestow punishment on you for the evil you have done," declares the LORD. "I myself will gather the remnant of my flock out of all the countries where I have driven them and will bring them back to their pasture, where they will be fruitful and increase in number. I will place shepherds over them who will tend them, and they will no longer be afraid or terrified, nor will any be missing," declares the LORD.

4. **God warns his people not to listen to the false prophets who say that he will not punish unrepentant sinners.**

Jer. 23:16–24.

Jer. 23:16–20. This is what the LORD Almighty says: "Do not listen to what the prophets are prophesying to you; they fill you with false hopes. They speak visions from their own minds, not from the mouth of the LORD. They keep saying to those who despise me, 'The LORD says: You will have peace.' And to all who follow the stubbornness of their hearts they say, 'No harm will come to you.' But which of them has stood in the council of the LORD to see or to hear his word? Who has listened and heard his word? See, the storm of the LORD will burst out in wrath, a whirlwind swirling down on the heads of the wicked. The anger of the LORD will not turn back until he fully accomplishes the purposes of his heart. In days to come you will understand it clearly."

Ezek. 13:1–16.

Ezek. 13:10–12. Because they lead my people astray, saying, "Peace," when there is no peace, and because, when a flimsy wall is built, they cover it with whitewash, therefore tell those who cover it with whitewash that it is going to fall. Rain will come in torrents, and I will send hailstones hurtling down, and violent winds will burst forth. When the wall collapses, will people not ask you, "Where is the whitewash you covered it with?"

5. **Jesus warns against false prophets who are wolves in sheep's clothing.**

Matt. 7:15. Watch out for false prophets. They come to you in sheep's clothing, but inwardly they are ferocious wolves.

6. **Paul warns that savage wolves will come, even from within the church, and will not spare the flock.**

Acts 29:29–31. I know that after I leave, savage wolves will come in among you and will not spare the flock. Even from your own number men will arise and distort the truth in order to draw away disciples after them. So be on your guard! Remember that for three years I never stopped warning each of you night and day with tears.

7. **Peter warns that false teachers will arise within the church and secretly introduce destructive heresies.**

2 Peter 2:1–3. There were also false prophets among the people, just as there will be false teachers among you. They will secretly introduce destructive heresies, even denying the sovereign Lord who bought them—bringing swift destruction on themselves. Many will follow their shameful ways and will bring the way of truth into disrepute. In their greed these teachers will exploit you with stories they have made up. Their condemnation has long been hanging over them, and their destruction has not been sleeping.

8. **False teachers masquerade also as angels of light.**

2 Cor. 11:1–15.

2 Cor. 11:13–15. Such men are false apostles, deceitful workmen, masquerading as apostles of Christ. And no wonder, for Satan himself masquerades as an angel of light. It is not surprising, then, if his servants masquerade as servants of righteousness. Their end will be what their actions deserve.

9. **Don't be like the Galatian Christians who were easily led away from the purity of the gospel by false teachers, the Judaizers.**

Gal. 3:1–9.

Gal. 3:1. You foolish Galatians! Who has bewitched you? Before your very eyes Jesus Christ was clearly portrayed as crucified.

10. **Test the spirits (by the word of God) to see whether or not they are from God.**

1 John 4:1–3.

1 John 4:1. Dear friends, do not believe every spirit, but test the spirits to see whether they are from God, because many false prophets have gone out into the world.

11. **Be like the Berean Christians.**

Acts 17:11. Now the Bereans were of more noble character than the Thessalonians, for they received the message with great eagerness and examined the Scriptures every day to see if what Paul said was true.

12. **Jesus commends the church that tests what it hears, and will not tolerate false teachers.**

    Rev. 2:2–3. *(To the church in Ephesus)* I know your deeds, your hard work and your perseverance. I know that you cannot tolerate wicked men, that you have tested those who claim to be apostles but are not, and have found them false. You have persevered and have endured hardships for my name, and have not grown weary.

13. **A horrible, shocking thing happened in Jeremiah's time. False prophets spread lies and the people loved it.**

    Jer. 5:30–31. A horrible and shocking thing has happened in the land: The prophets prophesy lies, the priests rule by their own authority, and my people love it this way. But what will you do in the end?

14. **God calls his people to repent and listen to the faithful prophets.**
    Jer. 6.
    Jer. 6:16–17. This is what the LORD says: "Stand at the crossroads and look; ask for the ancient paths, ask where the good way is, and walk in it and you will find rest for your souls. But you said, 'We will not walk in it.' I appointed watchmen over you and said, 'Listen to the sound of the trumpet!' But you said, 'We will not listen.'"

15. **Don't allow false teachers to entice you back into slavery to sin.**
    2 Peter 2:17–22.
    2 Peter 2:18–19. For they mouth empty, boastful words and, by appealing to the lustful desires of sinful human nature, they entice people who are just escaping from those who live in error. They promise them freedom, while they themselves are slaves of depravity—for a man is a slave to whatever has mastered him.

16. **Be on your guard so that you will not be carried away by lawless men.**

    2 Peter 3:17–18. Therefore, dear friends, since you already know this, be on your guard so that you may not be carried away by the error of lawless men and fall from your secure position. But grow in the grace and knowledge of our Lord and Savior Jesus Christ. To him be the glory both now and forever! Amen.

Fear

See also Comfort, p. 37; Prayer, p. 137; and Trust, p. 86.

1. **Believers need not be slaves to fear.**

    Rom. 8:15. You did not receive a spirit that makes you a slave again to fear, but you received the Spirit of sonship. And by him we cry, "Abba, Father."

    2 Tim. 1:7. God did not give us a spirit of timidity [fear], but a spirit of power, of love and of self-discipline.

2. **You need not be afraid if God is your helper.**

    Heb. 13:5–6. God has said, "Never will I leave you; never will I forsake you" [Deut. 31:6]. So we say with confidence, "The Lord is my helper; I will not be afraid. What can man do to me?" [Ps. 118:6–7].

3. **The Lord is the believer's light; he need not fear.**

    Ps. 27:1. The LORD is my light and my salvation—whom shall I fear? The LORD is the stronghold of my life—of whom shall I be afraid?

4. **Trust in God casts out fear.**

    Ps. 56:3–4. When I am afraid, I will trust in you. In God, whose word I praise, in God I trust; I will not be afraid. What can mortal man do to me?

    Ps. 56:10–11. In God, whose word I praise, in the LORD, whose word I praise—in God I trust; I will not be afraid.

5. **Do not fear those who can kill the body.**

    Matt. 10:28. Do not be afraid of those who kill the body but cannot kill the soul. Rather, be afraid of the one who can destroy both soul and body in hell.

6. **Don't be afraid; God cares for sparrows, and he will surely care for you.**

   Matt. 10:29–30. Are not two sparrows sold for a penny? Yet not one of them will fall to the ground apart from the will of your Father. And even the very hairs of your head are all numbered. So don't be afraid; you are worth more than many sparrows.

7. **Perfect love drives out fear.**

   1 John 4:18. There is no fear in love. But perfect love drives out fear, because fear has to do with punishment. The man who fears is not made perfect in love.

Forgiveness of Sins
(God's Forgiveness)

See also Salvation, p. 158.

1. **Believers are made as white as snow.**

    Isa. 1:18. "Come now, let us reason together," says the LORD. "Though your sins are like scarlet, they shall be as white as snow; though they are red as crimson, they shall be like wool."

2. **David sang joyfully after he repented of adultery and God forgave him.**

    Ps. 32:1–2. Blessed is he whose transgressions are forgiven, whose sins are covered. Blessed is the man whose sin the LORD does not count against him and in whose spirit is no deceit.

3. **David was depressed until he repented and was forgiven.**

    Ps. 32:3–4. When I kept silent, my bones wasted away through my groaning all day long. For day and night your hand was heavy upon me; my strength was sapped as in the heat of summer.

4. **God readily forgave David when he repented and confessed his sin.**

    Ps. 32:5. Then I acknowledged my sin to you and did not cover up my iniquity. I said, "I will confess my transgressions to the LORD"—and you forgave the guilt of my sin.

5. **David's confession of sin and his cry for forgiveness occurred only by God's grace.**

    Ps. 51:1–17.

6. God will not despise a broken spirit and contrite heart.

Ps. 51:17. The sacrifices of God are a broken spirit; a broken and contrite heart, O God, you will not despise.

7. How great is God's forgiveness!

Ps. 103:8–12. The LORD is compassionate and gracious, slow to anger, abounding in love. He will not always accuse, nor will he harbor his anger forever; he does not treat us as our sins deserve or repay us according to our iniquities. For as high as the heavens are above the earth, so great is his love for those who fear him; as far as the east is from the west, so far has he removed our transgressions from us.

8. The Lord is kind and forgiving.

Ps. 86:4–7. Bring joy to your servant, for to you, O LORD, I lift up my soul. You are kind and forgiving, O LORD, abounding in love to all who call to you. Hear my prayer, O LORD; listen to my cry for mercy. In the day of my trouble I will call to you, for you will answer me.

9. God calls sinners to seek him and promises them forgiveness when they repent.

Isa. 55:6–7. Seek the LORD while he may be found; call on him while he is near. Let the wicked forsake his way and the evil man his thoughts. Let him turn to the LORD, and he will have mercy on him, and to our God, for he will freely pardon.

10. Jesus extends a loving invitation.

Matt. 11:28–30. Come to me, all you who are weary and burdened, and I will give you rest. Take my yoke upon you and learn from me, for I am gentle and humble in heart and you will find rest for your souls. For my yoke is easy and my burden is light.

11. Jesus forgave the penitent woman.

Luke 7:36–50.

Luke 7:47–50. "Therefore, I tell you, her many sins have been forgiven—for she loved much. But he who has been forgiven little loves little." Then Jesus said to her, "Your sins are forgiven." The other guests began to say among themselves, "Who is this who even forgives sins?" Jesus said to the woman, "Your faith has saved you; go in peace."

12. **Jesus forgave the murderer on the cross (an example of one saved only by grace).**

    Luke 23:43. Jesus answered him, "I tell you the truth, today you will be with me in paradise."

13. **Sinners are forgiven when they repent and believe in Jesus.**

    Luke 15:11–32. *(the parable of the prodigal son)*

14. **Jesus tells us to pray for forgiveness.**

    Matt. 6:12. Forgive us our debts, as we also have forgiven our debtors.

15. **We are justified (cleared of all guilt) by faith in Jesus; in him we find peace.**

    Rom. 3:21–25. Now a righteousness from God, apart from law, has been made known, to which the Law and the Prophets testify. This righteousness from God comes through faith in Jesus Christ to all who believe. There is no difference, for all have sinned and fall short of the glory of God, and are justified freely by his grace through the redemption that came by Christ Jesus. God presented him as a sacrifice of atonement, through faith in his blood.

    Rom. 5:1. Since we have been justified through faith, we have peace with God through our Lord Jesus Christ. . . .

    Rom. 8:1, 4. There is now no condemnation for those who are in Christ Jesus. . . . [for those] who do not live according to the sinful nature but according to the Spirit.

16. **In love Jesus died to make us holy; we are without blemish.**

    Eph. 5:25–27. Husbands, love your wives, just as Christ loved the church and gave himself up for her to make her holy, cleansing her by the washing with water through the word, and to present her to himself as a radiant church, without stain or wrinkle or any other blemish, but holy and blameless.

    Heb. 10:10. By that will, we have been made holy through the sacrifice of the body of Jesus Christ once for all.

    Heb. 10:14. By one sacrifice he has made perfect forever those who are being made holy.

17. **The blood of Jesus Christ cleanses from all sin.**

    1 John 1:7. If we walk in the light, as he is in the light, we have fellowship with one another, and the blood of Jesus, his Son, purifies us from all sin.

18. **God graciously forgives when we confess our sins before him.**

1 John 1:9. If we confess our sins, he is faithful and just and will forgive us our sins and purify us from all unrighteousness.

Prov. 28:13–14. He who conceals his sins does not prosper, but whoever confesses and renounces them finds mercy. Blessed is the man who always fears the LORD, but he who hardens his heart falls into trouble.

19. **God forgives and saves all kinds of sinners, no matter how bad they are; he changes them.**

1 Cor. 6:9–11. Do you not know that the wicked will not inherit the kingdom of God? Do not be deceived: Neither the sexually immoral nor idolaters nor adulterers nor male prostitutes nor homosexual offenders nor thieves nor the greedy nor drunkards nor slanderers nor swindlers will inherit the kingdom of God. And that is what some of you were. But you were washed, you were sanctified, you were justified in the name of the Lord Jesus Christ and by the Spirit of our God.

20. **Zechariah had a vision of the high priest in filthy clothes, which were removed and replaced with pure white garments.**

Zech. 3:1–5. Then he showed me Joshua the high priest standing before the angel of the LORD, and Satan standing at his right side to accuse him. The LORD said to Satan, "The LORD rebuke you! Is not this man a burning stick snatched from the fire?" Now Joshua was dressed in the filthy clothes as he stood before the angel. The angel said to those who were standing before him, "Take off his filthy clothes." Then he said to Joshua, "See, I have taken away your sin and I will put rich garments on you." Then I said, "Put a clean turban on his head: So they put a clean turban on his head and clothed him while the angel of the LORD stood by.

21. **The Samaritan woman, an adulteress, was saved by Jesus; she received living water.**

John 4:4–26.

John 4:13–14. Jesus answered, "Everyone who drinks this water will be thirsty again, but whoever drinks the water I give him will never thirst. Indeed, the water I give him will become in him a spring of water welling up to eternal life."

22. **Peter, who denied Jesus, was forgiven and reinstated in his office.**

    John 21:15–19. *(Jesus even entrusted Peter with his precious people, for whom he died on the cross.)* Jesus said, "Feed my lambs. . . . Take care of my sheep."

23. **Jesus gave us the parable of the Pharisee and the tax collector.**

    Luke 18:9–14. *(The proud, self-righteous Pharisee was not justified, forgiven. But the humbled tax collector was justified and could go home with peace in his heart.)*

    Luke 18:13–14. The tax collector stood at a distance. He would not even look up to heaven, but beat his breast and said, "God, have mercy on me, a sinner." I tell you that this man, rather than the other, went home justified before God. For everyone who exalts himself will be humbled, and he who humbles himself will be exalted.

24. **Troubled sinners cry out for mercy, and God graciously forgives; he restores us to his love and favor.**

    Ps. 130.

    Ps. 130:3–4. If you, O LORD, kept a record of sins, O LORD, who could stand? But with you there is forgiveness; therefore you are feared.

25. **Believers are rescued from the dominion of darkness. They are brought into Jesus' eternal kingdom and are forgiven of all their sins.**

    Col. 1:13–14. He has rescued us from the dominion of darkness and brought us into the kingdom of the Son he loves, in whom we have redemption, the forgiveness of sins.

26. **God has lavished his grace on us, choosing us, forgiving us of all our sins through the shed blood of Christ.**

    Eph. 1:3–10.

    Eph. 1:7–8. In him we have redemption through his blood, the forgiveness of sins, in accordance with the riches of God's grace that he lavished on us with all wisdom and understanding.

27. **The prayer for forgiveness must be accompanied by repentance.**

    1 Kings 8:33–36, 46–53. *(Solomon, at the dedication of the temple, prayed that God would forgive his people if and when they should repent of their sin and sincerely serve him.)*

    1 Kings 8:33–36. When your people Israel have been defeated by an enemy because they have sinned against you, and when they

turn back to you and confess your name, praying and making supplication to you in this temple, then hear from heaven and forgive the sin of your people Israel and bring them back to the land you gave to their fathers. When the heavens are shut up and there is no rain because your people have sinned against you, and when they pray toward this place and confess your name and turn from their sin because you have afflicted them, then hear from heaven and forgive the sin of your servants, your people Israel. Teach them the right way to live, and send rain on the land you gave your people for an inheritance.

28. Nehemiah wept and confessed the sins of God's people.

Neh. 1:6–7. Let your ear be attentive and your eyes open to hear the prayer your servant is praying before you day and night for your servants, the people of Israel. I confess the sins we Israelites, including myself and my father's house, have committed against you. We have acted very wickedly toward you. We have not obeyed the commands, decrees and laws you gave your servant Moses.

29. God sweeps our sins away and wants us to sing for joy!

Isa. 44:22–23. "I have swept away your offenses like a cloud, your sins like the morning mist. Return to me, for I have redeemed you." Sing for joy, O heavens, for the LORD has done this; shout aloud, O earth beneath. Burst into song, you mountains, you forests and all your trees, for the LORD has redeemed Jacob, he displays his glory in Israel.

30. David prayed that the Lord would forgive the sins of his youth.

Ps. 25:7. Remember not the sins of my youth and my rebellious ways; according to your love remember me, for you are good, O LORD.

31. All the prophets testify that through faith in Jesus we have forgiveness of sins.

Acts 10:43. All the prophets testify about him that everyone who believes in him receives forgiveness of sins through his name.

32. Jesus is the only one through whom one can be saved and enjoy the forgiveness of sins.

Acts 4:12. Salvation is found in no one else, for there is no other name under heaven given to men by which we must be saved.

1 Tim. 2:5–6. For there is one God and one mediator between God and men, the man Christ Jesus, who gave himself as a ransom for all men—the testimony given in its proper time.

33. **Salvation, the forgiveness of sins, is only by grace, through faith in Jesus Christ.**

    Eph. 2:8–9. For it is by grace that you have been saved, through faith—and this not from yourselves, it is the gift of God—not by works, so that no one can boast.

34. **When people repent, and in faith seek the Lord, he graciously forgives their sins, hurls their iniquities, as it were, into the depths of the sea and remembers them no more.**

    Micah 7:18–19. Who is a God like you, who pardons sin and forgives the transgression of the remnant of his inheritance? You do not stay angry forever but delight to show mercy. You will again have compassion on us; you will tread our sins underfoot and hurl all our iniquities into the depths of the sea.

35. **God reconciles us to himself through Christ and counts our sins against us no more.**

    2 Cor. 5:18–19. All this is from God, who reconciled us to himself through Christ and gave us the ministry of reconciliation: that God was reconciling the world to himself in Christ, not counting men's sins against them.

Forgiving Others

1. **We must forgive our debtors.**

   Matt. 6:12. Forgive us our debts, as we also have forgiven our debtors.

2. **Forgiving others is an absolute necessity.**

   Matt. 6:14–15. If you forgive men when they sin against you, your heavenly Father will also forgive you. But if you do not forgive men their sins, your Father will not forgive your sins.

3. **Jesus says we must forgive often.**

   Matt. 18:21–22. Then Peter came to Jesus and asked, "Lord, how many times shall I forgive my brother when he sins against me? Up to seven times?" Jesus answered, "I tell you, not seven times, but seventy-seven times [or, seventy times seven]."

   Luke 17:3–4. If your brother sins, rebuke him, and if he repents, forgive him. If he sins against you seven times in a day, and seven times comes back to you and says, "I repent," forgive him.

4. **The parable of the unmerciful servant shows how sinful it is not to forgive; God sends judgment on this sin.**

   Matt. 18:23–25.

5. **Put away bitterness and anger; forgive as God forgives.**

   Eph. 4:31–32. Get rid of all bitterness, rage and anger, brawling and slander, along with every form of malice. Be kind and compassionate to one another, forgiving each other, just as in Christ God forgave you.

6. **Be imitators of God.**

   Eph. 5:1–2. Be imitators of God, therefore, as dearly loved children and live a life of love, just as Christ loved us and gave himself up for us as a fragrant offering and sacrifice to God.

7. **The father of the prodigal son forgave him and accepted him as completely as if he had not sinned. This father represents God. Thus Jesus reveals how God treats repentant sinners.**

   Luke 15:20–24.

8. **Jesus commands us to forgive others.**

   Mark 11:25. When you stand praying, if you hold anything against anyone, forgive him, so that your Father in heaven may forgive you your sins.

9. **Love keeps no record of wrongs.**

   1 Cor. 13:5. [Love] keeps no record of wrongs.

10. **Love covers (overlooks) a multitude of sins.**

    1 Peter 4:8. Above all, love each other deeply, because love covers over a multitude of sins.

11. **Restore with gentleness one who has fallen into sin.**

    Gal. 6:1. Brothers, if someone is caught in a sin, you who are spiritual should restore him gently. But watch yourself, or you also may be tempted.

12. **Paul tells us we must forgive and restore one who has sinned against us.**

    2 Cor. 2:5–11.

13. **Forgive a repentant sinner and affirm your love.**

    2 Cor. 2:7–8. Now, instead, you ought to forgive and comfort him, so that he will not be overwhelmed by excessive sorrow. I urge you, therefore, to reaffirm your love for him.

14. **When we forgive others, we outwit Satan.**

    2 Cor. 2:10–11. If you forgive anyone, I also forgive him. And what I have forgiven—if there was anything to forgive—I have forgiven in the sight of Christ for your sake, in order that Satan might not outwit us. For we are not unaware of his schemes.

15. **Joseph forgave his brothers for selling him into slavery and treated them kindly.**

    Gen. 45.

    Gen. 45:4–5. Then Joseph said to his brothers, "Come close to me." When they had done so, he said, "I am your brother Joseph, the one you sold into Egypt! And now, do not be distressed and do not be angry with yourselves for selling me here, because it was to save lives that God sent me ahead of you."

    Gen. 45:9–11. "Now hurry back to my father and say to him, '. . . You shall live in the region of Goshen and be near me—you, your children and grandchildren, your flocks and herds, and all you have. I will provide for you there, because five years of famine are still to come. Otherwise you and your household and all who belong to you will become destitute.'"

    Gen. 50:15–21.

    Gen. 50:19–21. Joseph said to them, "Don't be afraid. Am I in the place of God? You intended to harm me, but God intended it for good to accomplish what is now being done, the saving of many lives. So then, don't be afraid. I will provide for you and your children." And he reassured them and spoke kindly to them.

Friendships

1. Bad company corrupts good morals.

1 Cor. 15:33. Do not be misled: "Bad company corrupts good character."

2. Friends affect us for better or for worse.

Prov. 13:20. He who walks with the wise grows wise, but a companion of fools suffers harm.

3. A true friend favors us by a kind rebuke when it is needed.

Prov. 28:23. He who rebukes a man will in the end gain more favor than he who has a flattering tongue.

4. Stay away from a foolish man.

Prov. 14:7. Stay away from a foolish man, for you will not find knowledge on his lips.

5. Don't make friends with a hot-tempered man.

Prov. 22:24. Do not make friends with a hot-tempered man, do not associate with one easily angered. . . .

6. A true friend is one who may hurt you at times for your good.

Prov. 25:11–12. A word aptly spoken is like apples of gold in settings of silver. Like an earring of gold or an ornament of fine gold is a wise man's rebuke to a listening ear.

Prov. 27:6. The kisses of an enemy may be profuse, but faithful are the wounds of a friend.

7. A godly friend can be of great help.

Prov. 27:9. Perfume and incense bring joy to the heart, and the pleasantness of one's friend springs from his earnest counsel.

Prov. 27:17. As iron sharpens iron, so one man sharpens another.

8. Jonathan and David had an ideal friendship.

1 Sam. 20.

1 Sam. 20:17. Jonathan had David reaffirm his oath out of love for him, because he loved him as he loved himself.

1 Sam. 23:16. Saul's son Jonathan went to David at Horesh and helped him find strength in God.

9. Friendship with the world is hatred toward God.

James 4:4. You adulterous people, don't you know that friendship with the world is hatred toward God? Anyone who chooses to be a friend of the world becomes an enemy of God.

1 John 2:15–17. Do not love the world or anything in the world. If anyone loves the world, the love of the Father is not in him. For everything in the world—the cravings of sinful man, the lust of his eyes and the boasting of what he has and does—comes not from the Father but from the world. The world and its desires pass away, but the man who does the will of God lives forever.

Giving

1. Jesus heartily approved of the widow's small gift.

Luke 21:1–4. As he looked up, Jesus saw the rich putting their gifts into the temple treasury. He also saw a poor widow put in two very small copper coins. "I tell you the truth," he said, "this poor widow has put in more than all the others. All these people gave their gifts out of their wealth; but she out of her poverty put in all she had to live on."

2. The Lord wants us to give generously and cheerfully.

2 Cor. 8:1–9. *(the example of the Macedonian Christians)*

2 Cor. 8:1–5. Now, brothers, we want you to know about the grace that God has given the Macedonian churches. Out of the most severe trial, their overflowing joy and their extreme poverty welled up in rich generosity. For I testify that they gave as much as they were able, and even beyond their ability. Entirely on their own, they urgently pleaded with us for the privilege of sharing in this service to the saints. And they did not do as we expected, but they gave themselves first to the Lord and then to us in keeping with God's will.

2 Cor. 8:11–12. Now finish the work, so that your eager willingness to do it may be matched by your completion of it, according to your means. For if the willingness is there, the gift is acceptable according to what one has, not according to what he does not have.

2 Cor. 9:6–7. Remember this: Whoever sows sparingly will also reap sparingly, and whoever sows generously will also reap generously. Each man should give what he has decided in his heart to give, not reluctantly or under compulsion, for God loves a cheerful giver.

3. **Those who are rich must give accordingly.**

1 Tim. 6:17–19. Command those who are rich in this present world not to be arrogant nor to put their hope in wealth, which is so uncertain, but to put their hope in God, who richly provides us with everything for our enjoyment. Command them to do good, to be rich in good deeds, and to be generous and willing to share. In this way they will lay up treasure for themselves as a firm foundation for the coming age, so that they may take hold of the life that is truly life.

4. **Each Christian must give as the Lord has blessed.**

1 Cor. 16:1–2. Now about the collection for God's people: Do what I told the Galatian churches to do. On the first day of every week, each one of you should set aside a sum of money in keeping with his income, saving it up, so that when I come no collections will have to be made.

5. **Do not rob God of his tithes and offerings.**

Mal. 3:7–10. "Ever since the time of your forefathers you have turned away from my decrees and have not kept them. Return to me and I will return to you," says the LORD Almighty. "But you ask, 'How are we to return?' Will a man rob God? Yet you rob me. But you ask, 'How do we rob you?' In tithes and offerings. You are under a curse—the whole nation of you—because you are robbing me. Bring the whole tithe into the storehouse, that there may be food in my house. Test me in this," says the LORD Almighty, "and see if I will not throw open the floodgates of heaven and pour out so much blessing that you will not have room enough for it."

6. **Seek first the kingdom of God.**

Matt. 6:33. Seek first his kingdom and his righteousness, and all these things will be given to you as well.

7. **Don't give to be seen of men.**

Matt. 6:1–4. Be careful not to do your "acts of righteousness" before men, to be seen by them. If you do, you will have no reward from your Father in heaven. So when you give to the needy, do not announce it with trumpets, as the hypocrites do in the synagogues and on the streets, to be honored by men. I tell you the truth, they have received their reward in full. But when you give to the needy, do not let your left hand know what your right hand is doing, so that your giving may be in secret. Then your Father, who sees what is done in secret, will reward you.

8. God requires us to be merciful and give to the poor.

Prov. 14:21. He who despises his neighbor sins, but blessed is he who is kind to the needy.

Prov. 19:17. He who is kind to the poor lends to the LORD, and he will reward him for what he has done.

Prov. 22:9. A generous man will himself be blessed, for he shares his food with the poor.

Matt. 5:7. Blessed are the merciful, for they will be shown mercy.

Gal. 6:9–10. Let us not become weary in doing good, for at the proper time we will reap a harvest if we do not give up. Therefore, as we have opportunity, let us do good to all people, especially to those who belong to the family of believers.

9. To give to God's children is to give to Christ.

Matt. 24:34–46.

Matt. 25:35, 40. Then the King will say to those on his right, ". . . I was hungry and you gave me something to eat, I was thirsty and you gave me something to drink, I was a stranger and you invited me in. . . ." The King will reply, "I tell you the truth, whatever you did for one of the least of these brothers of mine, you did for me."

10. Be merciful and do good even to your enemies. Follow God's example.

Luke 6:27–36.

Luke 6:27–28. I tell you who hear me: Love your enemies, do good to those who hate you, bless those who curse you, pray for those who mistreat you.

11. Mere talk is not enough.

1 John 3:16–18. This is how we know what love is: Jesus Christ laid down his life for us. And we ought to lay down our lives for our brothers. If anyone has material possessions and sees his brother in need but has no pity on him, how can the love of God be in him? Dear children, let us not love with words or tongue but with actions and in truth.

12. **We see a good example in giving as King David, the leaders of Israel, and others gave willingly and liberally for the building of the house of God.**

    1 Chron. 29:1–9.

    1 Chron. 29:3. *(David sets an example.)* Besides, in my devotion to the temple of my God I now give my personal treasures of gold and silver for the temple of my God, over and above everything I have provided for this holy temple.

    1 Chron. 29:6. Then the leaders of families, the officers of the tribes of Israel, the commanders of thousands and commanders of hundreds, and the officials in charge of the king's work gave willingly.

    1 Chron. 29:9. The people rejoiced at the willing response of their leaders, for they had given freely and wholeheartedly to the LORD. David the king also rejoiced greatly.

13. **A generous giver will be blessed, but one who fails to give will suffer for it.**

    Prov. 11:24–25. One man gives freely, yet gains even more; another withholds unduly, but comes to poverty. A generous man will prosper; he who refreshes others will himself be refreshed.

14. **It is more blessed to give than to receive.**

    Acts 20:35. In everything I [Paul] did, I showed you [the elders at Ephesus] that by this kind of hard work we must help the weak, remembering the words the Lord Jesus himself said: "It is more blessed to give than to receive."

15. **Put first things first. Don't put off giving until you have what you want.**

    Hag. 1.

    Hag. 1:2–4. This is what the LORD Almighty says: "These people say, 'The time has not yet come for the LORD 's house to be built.' " Then the word of the LORD came through the prophet Haggai: "Is it a time for you yourselves to be living in your paneled houses, while this house remains a ruin?"

Homosexuality

To help homosexuals, see also Change, p. 117; Forgiveness of Sins, p. 72; Peace, p. 122; Overcoming Sin, p. 117; Repentance, p. 153; and Sexual Immorality, p. 177.

1. **God unequivocally forbids homosexual activity.**

   Lev. 18:22. Do not lie with a man as one lies with a woman; that is detestable.

2. **God condemned Sodom and Gomorrah for their homosexuality. It is sin.**

   Gen. 18:20–21. Then the LORD said, "The outcry against Sodom and Gomorrah is so great and their sin so grievous that I will go down and see if what they have done is as bad as the outcry that has reached me. If not, I will know."

3. **Sodom and Gomorrah were destroyed on account of their unrepentant homosexuality.**

   Gen. 19.

   Gen. 19:4–5. Before they had gone to bed, all the men from every part of the city of Sodom—both young and old—surrounded the house. They called to Lot, "Where are the men who came to you tonight? Bring them out to us so that we can have sex with them."

   Gen. 19:24–25. Then the LORD rained down burning sulfur on Sodom and Gomorrah—from the LORD out of the heavens. Thus he overthrew those cities and the entire plain, including all those living in the cities—and also the vegetation in the land.

4. **The example of Sodom and Gomorrah is given as a warning for people of all ages. God holds homosexuals fully accountable for their sin.**

   2 Peter 2:4–10.

   2 Peter 2:6–10. If he condemned the cities of Sodom and Gomorrah by burning them to ashes, and made them an example of what is going to happen to the ungodly; and if he rescued Lot, a righteous man, who was distressed by the filthy lives of lawless men (for that righteous man, living among them day after day, was tormented in his righteous soul by the lawless deeds he saw and heard)—if this is so, then the Lord knows how to rescue godly men from trials and to hold the unrighteous for the day of judgment, while continuing their punishment. This is especially true of those who follow the corrupt desire of the sinful nature and despise authority.

   Jude 6–7. And the angels who did not keep their positions of authority but abandoned their own home—these he has kept in darkness, bound with everlasting chains for judgment on the great Day. In a similar way, Sodom and Gomorrah and the surrounding towns gave themselves up to sexual immorality and perversion. They serve as an example of those who suffer the punishment of eternal fire.

5. **God's wrath is revealed against all of the godlessness and wickedness of men—including homosexuality.**

   Rom. 1:18–32.

6. **Paul describes homosexuality as a wicked perversion of God's gift.**

   Rom. 1:26–27. Because of this, God gave them over to shameful lusts. Even their women exchanged natural relations for unnatural ones. In the same way the men also abandoned natural relations with women and were inflamed with lust for one another. Men committed indecent acts with other men, and received in themselves the due penalty for their perversion.

7. **The wicked—including homosexuals—will not inherit the kingdom of God.**

   1 Cor. 6:9–10. Do you not know that the wicked will not inherit the kingdom of God? Do not be deceived: Neither the sexually immoral nor idolaters nor adulterers nor male prostitutes nor homosexual offenders nor thieves nor the greedy nor drunkards nor slanderers will inherit the kingdom of God.

8. There is hope for homosexuals—God forgives and cleanses persons of this sin.

1 Cor. 6:11. And that [homosexual offenders] is what some of you were. But you were washed, you were sanctified, you were justified in the name of the Lord Jesus Christ and by the Spirit of our God.

Hope

See also Trust, Faith in God, p. 186.

1. God has solutions to our problems.

    1 Cor. 10:13. No temptation has seized you except what is common to man. And God is faithful; he will not let you be tempted beyond what you can bear. But when you are tempted, he will also provide a way out so that you can stand up under it.

2. God's grace is sufficient for every need.

    2 Cor. 9:8. God is able to make all grace abound to you, so that in all things at all times, having all that you need, you will abound in every good work.

3. God is able to do more than we ask or imagine.

    Eph. 3:20. [God] . . . is able to do immeasurably more than all we ask or imagine, according to his power that is at work within us.

4. God is always faithful.

    Lam. 3:32. Though he brings grief, he will show compassion, so great is his unfailing love.

5. Hope is an anchor for the soul.

    Heb. 6:19–20. We have this hope as an anchor for the soul, firm and secure. It enters the inner sanctuary behind the curtain, where Jesus, who went before us, has entered on our behalf. He has become a high priest forever, in the order of Melchizedek.

6. Put your hope in God.

    Ps. 42.

Ps. 42:5. Why are you downcast, O my soul? Why so disturbed within me? Put your hope in God, for I will yet praise him, my Savior and my God.

7. Put your hope in a faithful and almighty God.

Ps. 146:3–10.

Ps. 146:5–6. Blessed is he whose help is the God of Jacob, whose hope is in the LORD his God, the Maker of heaven and earth, the sea, and everything in them—the LORD, who remains faithful forever.

8. Hope produces endurance and perseverance.

1 Thess. 1:3. We continually remember before our God and Father your work produced by faith, your labor prompted by love, and your endurance inspired by hope in our Lord Jesus Christ.

9. Believers have a living hope through the resurrection of Jesus Christ.

1 Peter 1:3. Praise be to the God and Father of our Lord Jesus Christ! In his great mercy he has given us new birth into a living hope through the resurrection of Jesus Christ from the dead.

10. Trusting in the God of hope will bring you yet more joy, peace, and hope.

Rom. 15:13. May the God of hope fill you with all joy and peace as you trust in him, so that you may overflow with hope by the power of the Holy Spirit.

Imitating Jesus

See also Loving and Serving Others, p. 96.

Note: An unbeliever cannot truly imitate Jesus. If one attempts to do so it will be a sham. No one can become a Christian by imitating Jesus. Salvation is only by grace through faith in Jesus Christ. But if you are a Christian you can and must imitate Him in the power of the Holy Spirit.

1. **Every Christian is predestined and called to become Christ-like.**

   Rom. 8:29–30. Those God foreknew he also predestined to be conformed to the likeness of his Son, that he might be the first-born among many brothers. And those he predestined, he also called; those he called, he also justified; those he justified, he also glorified.

2. **Christians are renewed in the image of God and are being transformed more and more into the likeness of Christ.**

   2 Cor. 3:18. We, who with unveiled faces all reflect the Lord's glory, are being transformed into his likeness with ever-increasing glory, which comes from the Lord, who is the Spirit.

   Col. 3:9–10. Do not lie to each other, since you have taken off your old self with its practices and have put on the new self, which is being renewed in knowledge in the image of its Creator.

   Eph. 4:22–24. You were taught, with regard to your former way of life, to put off your old self, which is being corrupted by its deceitful desires; to be made new in the attitude of your minds; and to put on the new self, created to be like God in true righteousness and holiness.

3. **We must imitate Jesus; we must walk as he walked.**

   1 John 2:6. Whoever claims to live in him must walk as Jesus did.

4. **Jesus calls us to become more like he is by imitating him.**

   John 13:2–11. *(Jesus purposely modeled for his disciples as he washed their feet.)*

   John 13:12–15. When he had finished washing their feet, he put on his clothes and returned to his place. "Do you understand what I have done for you?" he asked them. "You call me 'Teacher' and 'Lord,' and rightly so, for that is what I am. Now that I, your Lord and Teacher, have washed your feet, you also should wash one another's feet. I have set you an example that you should do as I have done for you."

5. **Paul instructs us to imitate Jesus in order to be a blessing to others.**

   Rom. 15:1–3. We who are strong ought to bear with the failings of the weak and not to please ourselves. Each of us should please his neighbor for his good, to build him up. For even Christ did not please himself but, as it is written: "The insults of those who insult you have fallen on me."

   Eph. 5:1–2. Be imitators of God, therefore, as dearly loved children and live a life of love, just as Christ loved us and gave himself up for us as a fragrant offering and sacrifice to God.

6. **When someone wrongs us, we must imitate Jesus and not retaliate or get revenge in any way. He set an example for us to follow.**

   1 Peter 2:18–23.

   1 Peter 2:20–21. How is it to your credit if you receive a beating for doing wrong and endure it? But if you suffer for doing good and you endure it, this is commendable before God. To this you were called, because Christ suffered for you, leaving you an example, that you should follow in his steps.

7. **Paul imitated Jesus so that he could be a good example for other Christians.**

   1 Cor. 11:1. Follow my example, as I follow the example of Christ.

8. **Thessalonian Christians soon became good models for others, partly by imitating Jesus and his disciples.**

1 Thess. 1:6–7. You became imitators of us and of the Lord; in spite of severe suffering, you welcomed the message with the joy given by the Holy Spirit. And so you became a model to all the believers in Macedonia and Achaia.

9. **Christ-like obedience is the way to a Christ-like enjoyment of divine love, and the way to have your joy made complete.**

    John 15:9–11. As the Father has loved me, so have I loved you. Now remain in my love. If you obey my commands, you will remain in my love, just as I have obeyed my Father's commands and remain in his love. I have told you this so that my joy may be in you and that your joy may be complete.

10. **The hope (certainty) of one day seeing Jesus face to face and being perfectly conformed to his image should motivate us to seek to be pure, even as he is pure.**

    1 John 3:2–3. Dear friends, now we are children of God, and what we will be has not yet been made known. But we know that when he appears, we shall be like him, for we shall see him as he is. Everyone who has this hope in him purifies himself, just as he is pure.

11. **The risen Savior lives to God. We who have died and risen with Christ must do the same.**

    Rom. 6:10–14.

    Rom. 6:10–12. The death he died, he died to sin once for all; but the life he lives, he lives to God. In the same way, count yourselves dead to sin but alive to God in Christ Jesus. Therefore do not let sin reign in your mortal body so that you obey its evil desires.

Loving and Serving Others

See also Church, Communion of Saints, p. 30; Imitating Jesus, p. 93; and Loving God, p. 101.

1. **Love one another in response to God's love for us.**

   1 John 4:9–21.

   1 John 4:9–11. This is how God showed his love among us: He sent his one and only Son into the world that we might live through him. This is love: not that we loved God, but that he loved us and sent his Son as an atoning sacrifice for our sins. Dear friends, since God so loved us, we also ought to love one another.

   1 John 4:21. He has given us this command: Whoever loves God must also love his brother.

2. **Love one another deeply.**

   1 Peter 1:22. Now that you have purified yourselves by obeying the truth so that you have sincere love for your brothers, love one another deeply, from the heart.

   1 Peter 4:8. Above all, love each other deeply, because love covers over a multitude of sins.

3. **Genuine love is serving others.**

   1 Peter 4:9–10. Offer hospitality to one another without grumbling. Each one should use whatever gift he has received to serve others, faithfully administering God's grace in its various forms.

4. **Love is absolutely essential; one is nothing without it.**

   1 Cor. 13:1–3.

5. **Paul describes what love really is.**

   1 Cor. 13:4–7. Love is patient, love is kind. It does not envy, it does not boast, it is not proud. It is not rude, it is not self-seeking, it is not easily angered, it keeps no record of wrongs. Love does not delight in evil but rejoices with the truth. It always protects, always trusts, always hopes, always perseveres.

6. **To love is to be devoted to one another.**

   Rom. 12:9–10. Love must be sincere. Hate what is evil; cling to what is good. Be devoted to one another in brotherly love. Honor one another above yourselves.

7. **By washing the disciples' feet, Jesus modeled for us, showing us how we must love one another.**

   John 13:2–17.

   John 13:14–15. Now that I, your Lord and Teacher, have washed your feet, you also should wash one another's feet. I have set you an example that you should do as I have done for you.

8. **Jesus commands us to love others in the manner in which he loved us, to imitate him.**

   Matt. 16:24. Then Jesus said to his disciples, "If anyone would come after me, he must deny himself and take up his cross and follow me."

   John 13:34. A new command I give you: Love one another. As I have loved you, so you must love one another.

   John 15:12. My command is this: Love each other as I have loved you.

9. **Don't be self-centered, but look out for others; in this imitate Jesus.**

   Phil. 2:3–5. Do nothing out of selfish ambition or vain conceit, but in humility consider others better than yourselves. Each of you should look not only to your own interests, but also to the interests of others. Your attitude should be the same as that of Christ Jesus. . . .

10. **Jesus gave his all for us.**

    Phil. 2:6–8.

11. **Do not seek honor and prestige but, like Jesus, be ready to serve others.**

    Matt. 20:20–28.

    Matt. 20:26–28. Whoever wants to become great among you must be your servant, and whoever wants to be first must be your slave—just as the Son of Man did not come to be served, but to serve, and to give his life as a ransom for many.

12. Attending to the needs of others is doing it for Christ.

Matt. 25:34–40.

Matt. 25:35–36. I was hungry and you gave me something to eat, I was thirsty and you gave me something to drink, I was a stranger and you invited me in, I needed clothes and you clothed me, I was sick and you looked after me, I was in prison and you came to visit me.

Matt. 25:40. I tell you the truth, whatever you did for one of the least of these brothers of mine, you did for me.

13. Don't become weary in doing good.

Gal. 6:9. Let us not become weary in doing good, for at the proper time we will reap a harvest if we do not give up.

14. Do good to all, especially to members of God's family.

Gal. 6:10. As we have opportunity, let us do good to all people, especially to those who belong to the family of believers.

15. Follow the golden rule.

Matt. 7:12. In everything, do to others what you would have them do to you, for this sums up the Law and the Prophets.

16. Don't be self-centered, but please others.

Rom. 15:1–2. We who are strong ought to bear with the failings of the weak and not to please ourselves. Each of us should please his neighbor for his good, to build him up.

17. Imitate Jesus.

Rom. 15:3. Even Christ did not please himself but, as it is written: "The insults of those who insult you have fallen on me."

18. Devote yourself to doing good.

Titus 3:14. Our people must learn to devote themselves to doing what is good, in order that they may provide for daily necessities and not live unproductive lives.

19. You can find your life by doing good.

Matt. 10:39. Whoever finds his life will lose it, and whoever loses his life for my sake will find it.

20. Love your enemies and those who persecute you.

Matt. 5:43–48. You have heard that it was said, "Love your neighbor and hate your enemy." But I tell you: Love your enemies and pray for those who persecute you, that you may be sons of your Father in heaven. He causes his sun to rise on the evil and the good, and sends rain on the righteous and the unrighteous. If you love those who love you, what reward will you get? Are not even the tax collectors doing that? And if you greet only your brothers, what are you doing more than others? Do not even pagans do that? Be perfect, therefore, as your heavenly Father is perfect.

Rom. 12:20–21. "If your enemy is hungry, feed him; if he is thirsty, give him something to drink. In doing this, you will heap burning coals on his head." Do not be overcome by evil, but overcome evil with good.

21. As members of Christ's body, we all need one another; each member must use his or her gifts to serve others.

1 Cor. 12:1–31.

1 Cor. 12:4–7. There are different kinds of gifts, but the same Spirit. There are different kinds of service, but the same Lord. There are different kinds of working, but the same God works all of them in all men. Now to each one the manifestation of the Spirit is given for the common good.

1 Peter. 4:10–11. Each one should use whatever gift he has received to serve others, faithfully administering God's grace in its various forms. If anyone speaks, he should do it as one speaking the very words of God. If anyone serves, he should do it with the strength God provides, so that in all things God may be praised through Jesus Christ. To him be the glory and the power for ever and ever. Amen.

22. True freedom is to serve one another in love.

Gal. 5:13–15. You, my brothers, were called to be free. But do not use your freedom to indulge the sinful nature; rather, serve one another in love. The entire law is summed up in a single command: "Love your neighbor as yourself." If you keep on biting and devouring each other, watch out or you will be destroyed by each other.

1 Thess. 4:9–11. Now about brotherly love we do not need to write to you, for you yourselves have been taught by God to love each other. And in fact, you do love all the brothers throughout

Macedonia. Yet we urge you, brothers, to do so more and more. Make it your ambition to lead a quiet life, to mind your own business and to work with your hands, just as we told you. . . .

23. Be a good Samaritan. Help needy persons whom the Lord puts in your pathway.

Luke 10:25–37. *(The parable of the Good Samaritan)*

Luke 10:36–37. Which of these three do you think was a neighbor to the man who fell into the hands of robbers? The expert replied, "The one who had mercy on him." Jesus told him, "Go and do likewise."

24. Mere talk and good intentions avail nothing. Act! Do good!

1 John 3:16–18. This is how we know what love is: Jesus Christ laid down his life for us. And we ought to lay down our lives for our brothers. If anyone has material possessions and sees his brother in need but has no pity on him, how can the love of God be in him? Dear children, let us not love with words or tongue but with actions and in truth.

James 2:15–17. Suppose a brother or sister is without clothes and daily food. If one of you says to him, "Go, I wish you well; keep warm and well fed," but does nothing about his physical needs, what good is it? In the same way, faith, by itself, if it is not accompanied by action, is dead.

25. You know the good you ought to do? Do it, lest you sin.

James 4:17. Anyone, then, who knows the good he ought to do and doesn't do it, sins.

Loving God

See also Obedience, p. 111; Loving and Serving Others, p. 96; Overcoming Sin, p. 117; and Progressive Sanctification, p. 141.

1. **The believer responds to God's love and favor.**

    Deut. 6:4–7. Hear, O Israel: The LORD our God, the LORD is one. Love the LORD your God with all your heart and with all your soul and with all your strength. These commandments that I give you today are to be upon your hearts. Impress them on your children. Talk about them when you sit at home and when you walk along the road, when you lie down and when you get up.

2. **Jesus calls us to love God above all else. He summarizes the Law as a matter of love.**

    Matt. 22:37–39. Jesus replied: "'Love the Lord your God with all your heart and with all your soul and with all your mind.' This is the first and greatest commandment. And the second is like it: 'Love your neighbor as yourself.' All the Law and the Prophets hang on these two commandments."

3. **Christ's love for us must compel us to love and serve him.**

    2 Cor. 5:14–15. Christ's love compels us, because we are convinced that one died for all, and therefore all died. And he died for all, that those who live should no longer live for themselves but for him who died for them and was raised again.

4. **Hold fast to the Lord and out of love keep his commandments.**

    Josh. 22:5. Be very careful to keep the commandment and the law that Moses the servant of the LORD gave you: to love the LORD your God, to walk in all his ways, to obey his commands, to hold fast to him and to serve him with all your heart and all your soul.

5. **To love Jesus is to obey his teaching.**

John 14:23–24. Jesus replied, "If anyone loves me, he will obey my teaching. My Father will love him, and we will come to him and make our home with him. He who does not love me will not obey my teaching. These words you hear are not my own; they belong to the Father who sent me."

6. **Solomon tells us to respond to God's favor by serving him from the heart.**

1 Kings 8:56–61.

1 Kings 8:61. Your hearts must be fully committed to the LORD our God, to live by his decrees and obey his commands, as at this time.

7. **David's charge to his son Solomon, to serve God with whole-hearted devotion, is good for all of us.**

1 Chron. 28:9. You, my son Solomon, acknowledge the God of your father, and serve him with wholehearted devotion and with a willing mind, for the LORD searches every heart and understands every motive behind the thoughts. If you seek him, he will be found by you; but if you forsake him, he will reject you forever.

8. **Motivated by love, reject partying and all sinful pleasures. Instead, put on Christ.**

Rom. 13:13–14. Let us behave decently, as in the daytime, not in orgies and drunkenness, not in sexual immorality and debauchery, not in dissension and jealousy. Rather, clothe yourselves with the Lord Jesus Christ, and do not think about how to gratify the desires of the sinful nature.

9. **God's love for us should move us to strive for purity.**

2 Cor. 7:1. Since we have these promises, dear friends, let us purify ourselves from everything that contaminates body and spirit, perfecting holiness out of reverence for God.

Lust, Evil Desires

1. Eve's sin began with lusting.

Gen. 3:6. When the woman saw that the fruit of the tree was good for food and pleasing to the eye, and also desirable for gaining wisdom, she took some and ate it. She also gave some to her husband, who was with her, and he ate it.

2. Don't covet.

Exod. 20:17. You shall not covet your neighbor's house. You shall not covet your neighbor's wife, or his manservant or maidservant, his ox or donkey, or anything that belongs to your neighbor.

3. Don't think about how to gratify the sinful nature.

Rom. 13:14. Clothe yourselves with the Lord Jesus Christ, and do not think about how to gratify the desires of the sinful nature.

4. Say no to ungodly passions.

Titus 2:11–12. The grace of God that brings salvation has appeared to all men. It teaches us to say "No" to ungodliness and worldly passions, and to live self-controlled, upright and godly lives in this present age.

5. Those who fulfill evil desires are objects of God's wrath.

Eph. 2:3. All of us also lived among them at one time, gratifying the cravings of our sinful nature and following its desires and thoughts. Like the rest, we are by nature objects of wrath.

6. Christ came to save us from lust and evil desires.

Eph. 2:4–5. Because of his great love for us, God, who is rich in mercy, made us alive with Christ even when we were dead in transgressions—it is by grace you have been saved.

7. **Don't conform to evil desires, but be holy.**

1 Peter 1:14–16. As obedient children, do not conform to the evil desires you had when you lived in ignorance. But just as he who called you is holy, so be holy in all you do; for it is written: "Be holy, because I am holy."

1 Peter 2:11. Dear friends, I urge you, as aliens and strangers in the world, to abstain from sinful desires, which war against your soul.

8. **Live by the Spirit to overcome the lusts of the flesh.**

Gal. 5:16. So I say, live by the Spirit, and you will not gratify the desires of the sinful nature.

9. **Those who live according to the sinful nature have their minds set on what that nature desires.**

Rom. 8:5–8. Those who live according to the sinful nature have their minds set on what that nature desires; but those who live in accordance with the Spirit have their minds set on what the Spirit desires. The mind of sinful man is death, but the mind controlled by the Spirit is life and peace; the sinful mind is hostile to God. It does not submit to God's law, nor can it do so. Those controlled by the sinful nature cannot please God.

Marriage, Husband/Wife Relationships

See also Peacemakers, Peacekeepers, p. 125.

1. **Marriage was instituted and designed by God.**
   Gen. 2:18–25.

2. **At the heart of marriage is companionship and intimacy, which both husband and wife must promote.**
   Gen. 2:18, 24. The LORD God said, "It is not good for the man to be alone. I will make a helper suitable for him." . . . For this reason a man will leave his father and mother and be united to his wife, and they will become one flesh.

3. **The relationship between husband and wife is similar to that between Christ and the church.**
   Eph. 5:23. The husband is the head of the wife as Christ is the head of the church, his body, of which he is the Savior.
   Eph. 5:31–32. "For this reason a man will leave his father and mother and be united to his wife, and the two will become one flesh." This is a profound mystery—but I am talking about Christ and the church.

4. **The husband is the head of the wife and the home.**
   Eph. 5:23. The husband is the head of the wife as Christ is the head of the church, his body, of which he is the Savior.

5. **Husbands must love their wives as Christ loved the church.**
   Eph. 5:25. Husbands, love your wives, just as Christ loved the church and gave himself up for her.

6. **Husbands must exercise headship in love.**

    Eph. 5:25–33.

    Col. 3:19. Husbands, love your wives and do not be harsh with them.

7. **Husbands must treat their wives with respect and as equal heirs of God's gifts.**

    1 Peter 3:7. Husbands, in the same way be considerate as you live with your wives, and treat them with respect as the weaker partner and as heirs with you of the gracious gift of life, so that nothing will hinder your prayers.

8. **The husband must manage his own home well; he is the manager.**

    1 Tim. 3:4. He must manage his own family well and see that his children obey him with proper respect.

9. **The husband and father is primarily responsible for training the children.**

    Eph. 6:4. Fathers, do not exasperate your children; instead, bring them up in the training and instruction of the Lord.

    See also Training Children, p. 182.

10. **God's design for the wife is that of a helper suitable for man.**

    Gen. 2:18. The LORD God said, "It is not good for the man to be alone. I will make a helper suitable for him."

11. **Both husband and wife must seek to reflect the relationship between Christ and his church.**

    Eph. 5:25, 32.

12. **A wife is to submit to her husband, as the church submits to Christ.**

    Eph. 5:22–24. Wives, submit to your husbands as to the Lord. For the husband is the head of the wife as Christ is the head of the church, his body, of which he is the Savior. Now as the church submits to Christ, so also wives should submit to their husbands in everything.

    Col. 3:18. Wives, submit to your husbands, as is fitting in the Lord.

    1 Peter 3:1–2. Wives, in the same way be submissive to your husbands so that, if any of them do not believe the word, they may be won over without talk by the behavior of their wives, when they see the purity and reverence of your lives.

13. **A woman is not to exercise authority over a man.**

   1 Tim. 2:11–14. A woman should learn in quietness and full submission. I do not permit a woman to teach or to have authority over a man; she must be silent. For Adam was formed first, then Eve. And Adam was not the one deceived; it was the woman who was deceived and became a sinner.

14. **The Bible gives a description of a wife of noble character, who uses her gifts faithfully.**

   Prov. 31:10–31.
   Prov. 31:10–11. A wife of noble character who can find? She is worth far more than rubies. Her husband has full confidence in her and lacks nothing of value.

15. **The fear of the Lord is more important than physical beauty.**

   Prov. 31:30. Charm is deceptive, and beauty is fleeting; but a woman who fears the LORD is to be praised.

   1 Peter 3:3–4. Your beauty should not come from outward adornment, such as braided hair and the wearing of gold jewelry and fine clothes. Instead, it should be that of your inner self, the unfading beauty of a gentle and quiet spirit, which is of great worth in God's sight.

16. **Husbands and wives must not fight and destroy each other.**

   Gal. 5:15. If you keep on biting and devouring each other, watch out or you will be destroyed by each other.

17. **Both husband and wife must quickly pursue peace when trouble arises.**

   Matt. 5:23–24. If you are offering your gift at the altar and there remember that your brother has something against you, leave your gift there in front of the altar. First go and be reconciled to your brother, then come and offer your gift.

   Rom. 12:18. If it is possible, as far as it depends on you, live at peace with everyone.

18. **A house divided against itself cannot stand.**

   Matt. 12:25. Jesus knew their thoughts and said to them, "Every kingdom divided against itself will be ruined, and every city or household divided against itself will not stand."

19. Keep loving those who are wayward.

2 Sam. 18:33. *(David never lost his love for his son Absalom, who tried to kill him. When he learned of his death, he wept.)* The king was shaken. He went up to the room over the gateway and wept. As he went, he said: "O my son Absalom! My son, my son Absalom! If only I had died instead of you—O Absalom, my son, my son!"

Mixed Marriages

1. Don't be yoked with an unbeliever.

2 Cor. 6:14–16. Do not be yoked together with unbelievers. For what do righteousness and wickedness have in common? Or what fellowship can light have with darkness? What harmony is there between Christ and Belial? What does a believer have in common with an unbeliever? What agreement is there between the temple of God and idols? For we are the temple of the living God. As God has said: "I will live with them and walk among them, and I will be their God, and they will be my people."

2. Two cannot walk together unless they are agreed.

Amos 3:3. Do two walk together unless they have agreed to do so?

3. There were sad results of mixed marriages prior to the flood.
Gen. 6:1–4.

4. God's people are warned against mixed marriages; unbelievers will lead them to sin.

Exod. 34:16. When you choose some of their daughters as wives for your sons and those daughters prostitute themselves to their gods, they will lead your sons to do the same.

Deut. 7:3–4. Do not intermarry with them [the heathen]. Do not give your daughters to their sons or take their daughters for your sons, for they will turn your sons away from following me to serve other gods, and the LORD's anger will burn against you and will quickly destroy you.

5. God will reveal his anger if and when his people marry unbelievers.

Josh. 23:12–13. If you turn away and ally yourselves with the survivors of these nations that remain among you and if you intermarry with them and associate with them, then you may be sure that the LORD your God will no longer drive out these nations before you. Instead, they will become snares and traps for you, whips on your backs and thorns in your eyes, until you perish from this good land, which the LORD your God has given you.

6. **In Ezra's time many did intermarry. This led to much sin, and Ezra confessed the guilt of God's people.**

   Ezra 9:1–15.

   Ezra 9:1–2. The leaders came to me [Ezra] and said, "The people of Israel . . . have taken some of their daughters as wives for themselves and their sons, and have mingled the holy race with the peoples around them. And the leaders and officials have led the way in this unfaithfulness."

7. **Men of Judah intermarried and were led into deep sin. God was angry with them.**

   Neh. 13:23–27. Moreover, in those days I saw men of Judah who had married women from Ashdod, Ammon and Moab. Half of their children spoke the language of Ashdod or the language of one of the other peoples, and did not know how to speak the language of Judah. I rebuked them and called curses down on them. I beat some of the men and pulled out their hair. I made them take an oath in God's name and said: "You are not to give your daughters in marriage to their sons, nor are you to take their daughters in marriage for your sons or for yourselves. Was it not because of marriages like these that Solomon king of Israel sinned? Among the many nations there was no king like him. He was loved by his God, and God made him king over all Israel, but even he was led into sin by foreign women. Must we hear now that you too are doing all this terrible wickedness and are being unfaithful to our God by marrying foreign women?"

Obedience, Keeping the Commandments

1. **Jesus requires obedience.**

   John 14:15. If you love me, you will obey what I command.

2. **Keeping the commandments of Jesus brings joy; you will remain in his love.**

   John 15:10–17.

3. **Stay on the straight and narrow path that leads to life; the broad path leads to death.**

   Matt. 7:13–14. Enter through the narrow gate. For wide is the gate and broad is the road that leads to destruction, and many enter through it. But small is the gate and narrow the road that leads to life, and only a few find it.

4. **Not all who say, "Lord, Lord," will enter God's kingdom.**

   Matt. 7:21. Not everyone who says to me, "Lord, Lord," will enter the kingdom of heaven, but only he who does the will of my Father who is in heaven.

5. **Jesus gave us the parable of the wise and foolish builders.**

   Matt. 7:24–27.

6. **God rewards obedience.**

   Prov. 13:13. He who scorns instruction will pay for it, but he who respects a command is rewarded.

7. To obey is better than sacrifice.

1 Sam. 15:22–23. Samuel replied: "Does the LORD delight in burnt offerings and sacrifices as much as in obeying the voice of the LORD? To obey is better than sacrifice, and to heed is better than the fat of rams. For rebellion is like the sin of divination, and arrogance like the evil of idolatry. Because you have rejected the word of the LORD, he has rejected you as king."

8. Listen to God's Word and do what it says.

Luke 11:28. Blessed rather are those who hear the word of God and obey it.

James 1:22–25; 2:14–26.

9. To love God is to keep his commandments.

1 John 5:2–3. This is how we know that we love the children of God: by loving God and carrying out his commands. This is love for God: to obey his commands. And his commands are not burdensome.

10. God's blessing and favor rest on those who obey him; obedience is the way to joy and peace.

Ps. 1.
Ps. 19:7–14.
Ps. 119:1–8.

11. If you truly know and love the Lord, you will want to keep his commands.

1 John 2:3–6. We know that we have come to know him if we obey his commands. The man who says, "I know him," but does not do what he commands is a liar, and the truth is not in him. But if anyone obeys his word, God's love is truly made complete in him. This is how we know we are in him: Whoever claims to live in him must walk as Jesus did.

1 John 5:2–4. This is how we know that we love the children of God: by loving God and carrying out his commands. This is love for God: to obey his commands. And his commands are not burdensome, for everyone born of God overcomes the world. This is the victory that has overcome the world, even our faith.

2 John 6. This is love: that we walk in obedience to his commands. As you have heard from the beginning, his command is that you walk in love.

12. **God teaches you the way to go, what is best for you, the way to peace.**

Isa. 48:17–19. This is what the LORD says—your Redeemer, the Holy One of Israel: "I am the LORD your God, who teaches you what is best for you, who directs you in the way you should go. If only you had paid attention to my commands, your peace would have been like a river, your righteousness like the waves of the sea. Your descendants would have been like the sand, your children like its numberless grains; their name would never be cut off nor destroyed from before me."

13. **God's promises should motivate us to live a life of purity and holiness.**

2 Cor. 7:1. Since we have these promises, dear friends, let us purify ourselves from everything that contaminates body and spirit, perfecting holiness out of reverence for God.

14. **Use your freedom in Christ, not to do evil but to serve him.**

Gal. 5:13. You, my brothers, were called to be free. But do not use your freedom to indulge the sinful nature; rather, serve one another in love.

15. **Swerve neither to the left nor to the right of the pathway of obedience.**

Prov. 4:25–27. Let your eyes look straight ahead, fix your gaze directly before you. Make level paths for your feet and take only ways that are firm. Do not swerve to the right or the left; keep your foot from evil.

Overcoming Evil
(How to Handle It When Others Wrong You)

1. **Seek to communicate privately with the person who has wronged you.**

    Matt. 18:15. If your brother sins against you, go and show him his fault, just between the two of you. If he listens to you, you have won your brother over.

2. **If you can't get the matter settled, take one or two with you.**

    Matt. 18:16. If he will not listen, take one or two others along, so that "every matter may be established by the testimony of two or three witnesses."

3. **If that doesn't work, tell it to the church; seek help there.**

    Matt. 18:17. If he refuses to listen to them, tell it to the church; and if he refuses to listen even to the church, treat him as you would a pagan or a tax collector.

4. **Bless those who persecute you.**

    Rom. 12:14. Bless those who persecute you; bless and do not curse.

5. **Paul tells how to overcome evil and how to react when someone wrongs you.**

    Rom. 12:17–21.

6. **Do not seek revenge.**

    Rom. 12:17. Do not repay anyone evil for evil. Be careful to do what is right in the eyes of everybody.

Rom. 12:19. Do not take revenge, my friends, but leave room for God's wrath, for it is written: "It is mine to avenge; I will repay," says the LORD.

Prov. 20:22. Do not say, "I'll pay you back for this wrong!" Wait for the Lord, and he will deliver you.

7. Pursue peace with everyone.

Rom. 12:18. If it is possible, as far as it depends on you, live at peace with everyone.

8. Overcome evil with good.

Rom. 12:21. Do not be overcome by evil, but overcome evil with good.

9. Imitate Jesus by suffering wrongfully, if need be; in no way should you try to get even.

1 Peter 2:18–23.

1 Peter 2:19–23. For it is commendable if a man bears up under the pain of unjust suffering because he is conscious of God. But how is it to your credit if you receive a beating for doing wrong and endure it? But if you suffer for doing good and you endure it, this is commendable. To this you were called, because Christ suffered for you, leaving you an example, that you should follow in his steps. "He committed no sin, and no deceit was found in his mouth." When they hurled their insults at him, he did not retaliate; when he suffered, he made no threats. Instead, he entrusted himself to him who judges justly.

1 Peter 3:8–9. Finally, all of you, live in harmony with one another; be sympathetic, love as brothers, be compassionate and humble. Do not repay evil with evil or insult with insult, but with blessing, because to this you were called so that you may inherit a blessing.

10. Love your enemies and do good to them.

Matt. 5:43–47.

Rom. 12:20. If your enemy is hungry, feed him; if he is thirsty, give him something to drink. In doing this, you will heap burning coals on his head.

11. Turn the other cheek; be kind to the person who has wronged you.

Matt. 5:38–42.

115

1 Thess. 5:15. Make sure that nobody pays back wrong for wrong, but always try to be kind to each other and to everyone else.

12. Do not testify against your neighbor, nor seek revenge.

Prov. 24:28–29. Do not testify against your neighbor without cause, or use your lips to deceive. Do not say, "I'll do to him as he has done to me; I'll pay that man back for what he did."

13. Moses gives a practical example of what to do after someone has wronged you.

Exod. 23:4–5. If you come across your enemy's ox or donkey wandering off, be sure to take it back to him. If you see the donkey of someone who hates you fallen down under its load, do not leave it there; be sure you help him with it.

Overcoming Sin, Changing
(to Please God and Resolve Problems)

See also Progressive Sanctification, p. 141; and Repentance, p. 153.

1. **True Christians can change, for God makes it possible through a spiritual renewal.**

    2 Cor. 5:17. Therefore, if anyone is in Christ, he is a new creation; the old has gone, the new has come!

    Ezek. 36:25–27. I will sprinkle clean water on you, and you will be clean; I will cleanse you from all your impurities and from all your idols. I will give you a new heart and put a new spirit in you; I will remove from you your heart of stone and give you a heart of flesh. And I will put my Spirit in you and move you to follow my decrees and be careful to keep my laws.

2. **Believers are children of God, born again by the Holy Spirit.**

    John 1:12–13. Yet to all who received him, to those who believed in his name, he gave the right to become children of God—children born not of natural descent, nor of human decision or of a husband's will, but born of God.

    Titus 3:4–6. But when the kindness and love of God our Savior appeared, he saved us, not because of righteous things we had done, but because of his mercy. He saved us through the washing of rebirth and renewal by the Holy Spirit, whom he poured out on us generously through Jesus Christ our Savior.

3. **All Christians are called to live by the Holy Spirit, who dwells in us and empowers us to overcome sin and lead a godly life.**

    Rom 8:1–14.

Rom. 8:9. You, however, are controlled not by the sinful nature but by the Spirit, if the Spirit of God lives in you. And if anyone does not have the Spirit of Christ, he does not belong to Christ.

Rom. 8:13–14. For if you live according to the sinful nature, you will die; but if by the Spirit you put to death the misdeeds of the body, you will live, because those who are led by the Spirit of God are sons of God.

4. **God calls us to work out our salvation in every area of life. We need not go it on our own. God enables us to do so.**

   Phil. 2:12–13. Therefore, my dear friends, as you have always obeyed—not only in my presence, but now much more in my absence—continue to work out your salvation with fear and trembling, for it is God who works in you to will and act according to his good purpose.

5. **God has given us all we need for life and godliness.**

   2 Peter 1:3. His divine power has given us everything we need for life and godliness through our knowledge of him who called us by his own glory and goodness.

6. **God will make all grace abound to you, so that you can overcome any specific sin and do his will.**

   2 Cor. 9:8. And God is able to make all grace abound to you, so that in all things at all times, having all that you need, you will abound in every good work.

7. **A true Christian will not continue to live in sin.**

   1 John 3:4–10.

   1 John 3:6. No one who lives in him keeps on sinning. No one who continues to sin has either seen him or known him.

   1 John 3:9. No one who is born of God will continue to sin, because God's seed remains in him; he cannot go on sinning, because he has been born of God.

8. **By nature we are slaves to sin. Jesus came to set us free.**

   John 8:31–36.

   John 8:34–36. Jesus replied, "I tell you the truth, everyone who sins is a slave to sin. Now a slave to sin has no permanent place in the family, but a son belongs to it forever. So if the Son sets you free, you will be free indeed.

9. **Christians are set free so that we may be slaves to righteousness.**

   Rom. 6:15–18. What then? Shall we sin because we are not under law but under grace? By no means! Don't you know that when you offer yourselves to someone to obey him as slaves, you are slaves to the one whom you obey—whether you are slaves to sin, which leads to death, or to obedience, which leads to righteousness? But thanks be to God that, though you used to be slaves to sin, you wholeheartedly obeyed the form of teaching to which you were entrusted. You have been set free from sin and have become slaves to righteousness.

10. **We must keep working to overcome sin and use our bodies to serve the Lord only.**

    Rom. 6:19–23.

11. **In response to God's saving grace keep putting off old sinful ways and putting on new and godly ways.**

    Eph. 4:22–24. You were taught, with regard to your former way of life, to put off your old self, which is being corrupted by its deceitful desires; to be made new in the attitude of your minds; and to put on the new self, created to be like God in true righteousness and holiness.

12. **The apostle Paul gives us specific instructions on what must be done.**

    Eph. 4:25– 5:21.
    Col. 3:1–17.

13. **We are directed to live by the Spirit and put off the acts of the sinful nature and seek the fruit of the Spirit.**

    Gal. 5:16–26.
    Gal. 5:19–26. The acts of the sinful nature are obvious: sexual immorality, impurity and debauchery; idolatry and witchcraft; hatred, discord, jealousy, fits of rage, selfish ambition, dissensions, factions and envy; drunkenness, orgies, and the like. I warn you, as I did before, that those who live like this will not inherit the kingdom of God. But the fruit of the Spirit is love, joy, peace, patience, kindness, goodness, faithfulness, gentleness and self-control. Against such things there is no law. Those who belong to Christ Jesus have crucified the sinful nature with its passions and desires. Since we live by

the Spirit, let us keep in step with the Spirit. Let us not become conceited, provoking and envying each other.

14. **Adulterers, drunkards, homosexuals and others regarded by many as having incurable diseases can by God's power and grace overcome their sin.**

    1 Cor. 6:9–11. For we know that since Christ was raised from the dead, he cannot die again; death no longer has mastery over him. The death he died, he died to sin once and for all; but the life he lives he lives to God. In the same way, count yourselves dead to sin but alive to God in Christ Jesus.

15. **Do not allow yourself to be mastered by any sin.**

    1 Cor. 6:12. "Everything is permissible for me"—but not everything is beneficial. "Everything is permissible for me"—but I will not be mastered by anything.

    2 Peter 2:19. They [false teachers] promise them freedom, while they themselves are slaves of depravity—for a man is a slave to whatever has mastered him.

16. **Use the whole armor of God as you fight the spiritual battle.**

    Eph. 6:10–18.

    Eph. 6:10–11. Finally, be strong in the Lord and in his mighty power. Put on the full armor of God so that you can take your stand against the devil's schemes.

17. **Be vigilant! Your adversary, the devil, would like to devour you.**

    1 Peter 5:8–9. Be self-controlled and alert. Your enemy the devil prowls around like a roaring lion looking for someone to devour. Resist him, standing firm in the faith, because you know that your brothers throughout the world are undergoing the same kind of sufferings.

18. **Resist the devil, who wants to keep you in bondage to sin.**

    James 4:17. Anyone, then, who knows the good he ought to do and doesn't do it, sins.

19. **The devil may get others to entice you. If and when this happens resolutely refuse to consent.**

    Prov. 1:10–19.

    Prov. 1:10. My son, if sinners entice you, do not give in to them.

20. Stand firm; don't vacillate; don't be moved.

1 Cor. 15:58. Therefore my dear brothers, stand firm. Let nothing move you. Always give yourselves fully to the work of the Lord, because you know that your labor in the Lord is not in vain.

21. Studiously avoid the path of the wicked; turn from it.

Prov. 4:14–15. Do not set foot on the path of the wicked or walk in the way of evil men. Avoid it, do not travel on it; turn from it and go on your way.

22. Pray earnestly, fervently for God to give you victory over sinful thoughts, words and deeds, as did the Psalmist.

Ps. 19:12–14. Who can discern his errors? Forgive my hidden faults. Keep your servant also from willful sins; may they not rule over me. Then will I be blameless, innocent of transgression. May the words of my mouth and the meditation of my heart be pleasing in your sight O LORD, my Rock and my Redeemer.

For more on this see also Progressive Sanctification, p. 141.

Peace, Rest

See also Conscience, p. 44.

1. **Christ gives peace and rest to all who come to him in faith.**

    Matt. 11:28–30. Come to me, all you who are weary and burdened, and I will give you rest. Take my yoke upon you and learn from me, for I am gentle and humble in heart, and you will find rest for your souls. For my yoke is easy and my burden is light.

2. **Peace comes through justification by faith in Jesus.**

    Rom. 5:1. Since we have been justified through faith, we have peace with God through our Lord Jesus Christ.

3. **Jesus gives us peace.**

    John 14:27. Peace I leave with you; my peace I give you. I do not give to you as the world gives. Do not let your hearts be troubled and do not be afraid.

4. **Jesus was punished for our sins so that we may have peace.**

    Isa. 53:5. The punishment that brought us peace was upon him, and by his wounds we are healed.

5. **The penitent woman, who wept at Jesus' feet, found peace through him.**

    Luke 7:36–50.
    Luke 7:48. Then Jesus said to her, "Your sins are forgiven."
    Luke 7:50. Jesus said to the woman, "Your faith has saved you; go in peace."

6. **Humble trust in the Lord gives peace.**

    Ps. 4:8. I will lie down and sleep in peace, for you alone, O LORD, make me dwell in safety.

7. **God promises peace to his people.**

    Ps. 85:8. I will listen to what God the LORD will say; he promises peace to his people, his saints—but let them not return to folly.

8. **Peace is the result of being controlled by the Spirit.**

    Rom. 8:6. The mind of sinful man is death, but the mind controlled by the Spirit is life and peace.

9. **Peace is the fruit of the Spirit.**

    Gal. 5:22–23. The fruit of the Spirit is love, joy, peace, patience, kindness, goodness, faithfulness, gentleness and self-control.

10. **God gives peace to those whose minds are fixed on him.**

    Isa. 26:3–4. You will keep in perfect peace him whose mind is steadfast, because he trusts in you. Trust in the LORD forever, for the LORD, the LORD, is the Rock eternal.

11. **The peace of God comes through praying in faith.**

    Phil. 4:6–7. Do not be anxious about anything, but in everything, by prayer and petition, with thanksgiving, present your requests to God. And the peace of God, which transcends all understanding, will guard your hearts and your minds in Christ Jesus.

12. **Jesus is the Prince of Peace.**

    Isa. 9:6. He will be called Wonderful Counselor, Mighty God, Everlasting Father, Prince of Peace.

13. **Those who walk uprightly enter into peace.**

    Isa. 57:2. Those who walk uprightly enter into peace; they find rest as they lie in death.

14. **God revives, heals, and gives peace to those who are contrite.**

    Isa. 57:14–21.

    Isa. 57:19–20. "Peace, peace, to those far and near," says the LORD. "And I will heal them." But the wicked are like the tossing sea, which cannot rest, whose waves cast up mire and mud.

15. **There is no peace for the wicked.**

    Isa. 57:21. "There is no peace," says my God, "for the wicked."

16. False prophets will say, "Peace, peace," when there is no peace.

Jer. 8:11–12. They dress the wound of my people as though it were not serious. "Peace, peace," they say, when there is no peace. Are they ashamed of their loathsome conduct? No, they have no shame at all; they do not even know how to blush. So they will fall among the fallen; they will be brought down when they are punished, says the LORD.

Peacemakers, Peacekeepers

See also Forgiving Others, p. 79.

Note: Texts are listed which give instructions concerning peacemakers, peacekeeping, and promoting peace, harmony and unity. It is important to remember that living by these instructions begins in the home and among extended family members.

1. **Jesus declares peacemakers to be blessed.**

   Matt. 5:9. Blessed are the peacemakers, for they will be called the sons of God.

2. **Make every effort, do all you can, to live at peace with everyone.**

   Heb. 12:14. Make every effort to live at peace with all men and to be holy; without holiness no one will see the Lord.

   Rom. 12:18. If it is possible, as far as it depends on you, live at peace with everyone.

3. **Seek peace and pursue it, speaking no evil or lies.**

   Ps. 34:13–14. Keep your tongue from evil and your lips from speaking lies. Turn from evil and do good; seek peace and pursue it.

4. **Wisdom from God is peace loving.**

   James 3:17–18. But the wisdom that comes from heaven is first of all pure; then peace-loving, considerate, submissive, full of mercy and good fruit, impartial and sincere. Peacemakers who sow in peace raise a harvest of righteousness.

5. **Aim for perfection, be of one mind, live in peace.**

   2 Cor. 13:11. Finally, my brothers, good-by. Aim for perfection, listen to my appeal, be of one mind, live in peace. And the God of love and peace will be with you.

6. **God takes delight in seeing his children living together in unity. Ps. 133:1–3.**

   Ps. 133:1. How good and pleasant it is when brothers live in unity!

7. **If someone has something against you and your relationship is strained or broken, you must take the initiative to become reconciled. It is even more urgent than being in church on Sunday.**

   Matt. 5:23–24. Therefore, if you are offering your gift at the altar and remember that your brother has something against you, leave your gift there in front of the altar. First go and be reconciled to your brother, then come and offer your gift.

8. **If someone has sinned against you, you must take the initiative to get the matter cleared up, to restore peace.**

   Matt. 18:15. If your brother sins against you, go and show him his fault, just between the two of you. If he listens to you, you have won your brother over.

9. **If that person will not listen to you, seek the help of one or two other believers.**

   Matt. 18:16. But if he will not listen, take one or two others along, so that every matter may be established by the testimony of two or three witnesses.

10. **If he will not listen to them tell it to the church.**

    Matt. 18:17. If he refuses to listen to them, tell it to the church; and if he refuses to listen even to the church, treat him as you would a pagan or a tax collector.

11. **To promote peace, harmony and unity, love one another from the heart. Overlook many offenses, sins.**

    1 Peter 1:22–23. Now that you have purified yourselves by obeying the truth so that you have sincere love for your brothers, love one another deeply, from the heart. For you have been born again, not of perishable seed, but of imperishable, through the living and enduring word of God.

    1 Peter 4:8. Above all, love each other deeply, because love covers over a multitude of sins.

12. **Peter gives other ways by which we can promote peace and harmony.**

   1 Peter 3:8–11. Finally, all of you, live in harmony with one another; be sympathetic, love as brothers, be compassionate and humble. Do not repay evil with evil or insult with insult, but blessing with blessing, because to this you were called so that you may inherit a blessing. For, "Whosoever would love life and see good days must keep his tongue from evil and his lips from deceitful speech. He must turn from evil and do good; he must seek peace and pursue it."

13. **Use your God-given freedom to serve one another and avoid bitter strife.**

   Gal. 5:13–15. You, my brothers, were called to be free. But do not use your freedom to indulge the sinful nature; rather, serve one another in love. The entire law is summed up in a single command: "Love your neighbor as yourself." If you keep on biting and devouring each other, watch out or you will be destroyed by each other.

14. **Put off the deeds of the sinful nature which destroy peace and harmony.**

   Gal. 5:19–20. The acts of sinful nature are obvious: sexual immorality, impurity and debauchery; idolatry and witchcraft; hatred, discord, jealousy, fits of rage, selfish ambition, dissensions, factions. . . .

   Gal. 5:22–23. But the fruit of the spirit is love, joy, peace, patience, kindness, goodness, faithfulness, gentleness and self-control. Against such things there is no law.

15. **Follow the golden rule given by Jesus.**

   Matt. 7:12. So in everything, do to others what you would have them do to you, for this sums up the Law and the Prophets.

16. **Be patient. Bear with one another.**

   Prov. 15:18. A hot-tempered man stirs up dissension, but a patient man calms a quarrel.

   Prov 20:3. It is to a man's honor to avoid strife, but every fool is quick to quarrel.

   Prov. 26:21. As charcoal to embers and as wood to fire, so is a quarrelsome man for kindling strife.

   1 Cor. 13:4. Love is patient, love is kind. It does not envy, it does not boast, it is not proud.

17. **An angry person causes dissension.**

Prov. 29:22. An angry man stirs up dissension, and a hot-tempered one commits many sins.

18. **Stirring up another person's anger also produces strife.**

Prov. 30:33. For as churning the milk produces butter, and as twisting the nose produces blood, so stirring up anger produces strife.

19. **Put on other Christ-like virtues which promote peace.**

Col. 3:12–13. May the Lord make your love increase and overflow for each other and for everyone else, just as ours does for you. May he strengthen your hearts so that you will be blameless and holy in the presence of our God and Father when our Lord Jesus comes with all his holy ones.

20. **Peacefully accept God-ordained diversity within basic unity.**

Eph. 4:1–16.

Eph. 4:2–6. Be completely humble and gentle; be patient, bearing with one another in love. Make every effort to keep the unity of the Spirit through the bond of peace. There is one body and one Spirit—just as you were called to one hope when you were called.

21. **Avoid judging one another in disputable matters.**

Rom. 14:1–23.

Rom. 14:1. Accept him whose faith is weak, without passing judgment on disputable matters.

Rom. 14:19. Let us therefore make every effort to do what leads to peace and to mutual edification.

22. **Communicate in a manner that promotes peace.**

Eph. 4:15. Instead, speaking the truth in love, we will in all things grow up into him who is the Head, that is, Christ.

Eph. 4:29. Do not let any unwholesome talk come out of your mouths, but only what is helpful for building others up according to their needs, that it may benefit those who listen.

23. **Accept others in the spirit of unity even while you strongly disagree with them on disputable matters. The primary goal is to glorify the Lord.**

Rom.15:5–7. May the God who gives you endurance and encouragement give you a spirit of unity among yourselves as you follow

Christ Jesus, so that with one heart and mouth you may glorify the God and Father of our Lord Jesus Christ. Accept one another, then, just as Christ accepted you, in order to bring praise to God.

24. **If a legal dispute develops between you and another Christian, do not turn to unbelievers for help. Rather seek the help of one or more fellow Christians.**

1 Cor. 6:1–8.

1 Cor. 6:1. If any of you has a dispute with another, dare he take it before the ungodly for judgment instead of before the saints?

1 Cor. 6:4–6. Therefore, if you have disputes about such matters, appoint as judges even men of little account in the church! I say this to shame you. Is it possible that there is nobody among you wise enough to judge a dispute between believers? But instead, one brother goes to law against another—and this in front of unbelievers!

25. **Be willing to suffer wrongfully rather than to take another Christian to court.**

1 Cor. 6:7. The very fact that you have lawsuits among you means you have been completely defeated already. Why not rather be wronged? Why not rather be cheated?

26. **Get rid of those traits that cause enmity and dissension.**

Eph. 4:31. Get rid of all bitterness, rage and anger, brawling and slander, along with every form of malice.

27. **Forgive those who have sinned against you. Forgive as God forgave you. That is, in the manner God forgave you. Imitate God in forgiving others. There is no peace, no reconciliation apart from forgiveness.**

Eph. 4:32. Be kind and compassionate to one another, forgiving each other, just as in Christ God forgave you.

Eph. 5:1–2. Be imitators of God, therefore, as dearly loved children and live a life of love, just as Christ loved us and gave himself for us as a fragrant offering and sacrifice to God.

Persecution

Note: Suffering persecution is being maltreated by others because you are a true disciple of Christ. It includes being falsely accused, unjustly condemned or imprisoned, being ridiculed, scorned, rejected, or injured. Persecution is not suffering for doing wrong toward others or for disobeying rightful authority.

1. **Why do people persecute Christians, even when they are doing good?**

    John 15:18–21. If the world hates you, keep in mind that it hated me first. If you belonged to the world, it would love you as its own. As it is, you do not belong to the world, but I have chosen you out of the world. That is why the world hates you. Remember the words I spoke to you: "No servant is greater than his master." If they persecuted me, they will persecute you also. If they obeyed my teaching, they will obey yours also. They will treat you this way because of my name, for they do not know the One who sent me.

    2 Tim. 3:10–14. You, however, know all about my teaching, my way of life, my purpose, faith, patience, love, endurance, persecutions, sufferings—what kinds of things happened to me in Antioch, Iconium and Lystra, the persecutions I endured. Yet the Lord rescued me from all of them. In fact, everyone who wants to live a godly life in Christ Jesus will be persecuted, while evil men and impostors will go from bad to worse, deceiving and being deceived. But as for you, continue in what you have learned and have become convinced of, because you know those from whom you learned it.

    1 John 3:1. How great is the love the Father has lavished on us, that we should be called children of God! And that is what we are! The reason the world does not know us is that it did not know him.

2. **Cain persecuted his brother Abel because his own works were evil, while Abel's were righteous.**

Gen. 4:2–7.

1 John 3:12–14. Do not be like Cain, who belonged to the evil one and murdered his brother. And why did he murder him? Because his own actions were evil and his brother's were righteous. Do not be surprised, my brothers, if the world hates you. We know that we have passed from death to life, because we love our brothers. Anyone who does not love remains in death.

3. **Do good to and pray for those who persecute you. Love your enemies.**

Matt. 5:38–42. You have heard that it was said, "Eye for eye, and tooth for tooth." But I tell you, Do not resist an evil person. If someone strikes you on the right cheek, turn to him the other also. And if someone wants to sue you and take your tunic, let him have your cloak as well. If someone forces you to go one mile, go with him two miles. Give to the one who asks you, and do not turn away from the one who wants to borrow from you.

Matt. 5:43–48.

Matt. 5:43–45. You have heard that it was said, "Love your neighbor and hate your enemy." But I tell you: Love your enemies and pray for those who persecute you, that you may be sons of your Father in heaven. He causes his sun to rise on the evil and the good, and sends rain on the righteous and the unrighteous.

Rom. 12:14. Bless those who persecute you; bless and do not curse.

4. **Imitate Stephen, who prayed for his persecutors as they were stoning him.**

Acts 7:60. Then he fell on his knees and cried out, "Lord, do not hold this sin against them." When he had said this, he fell asleep.

5. **In dealing with your persecutors be wise and innocent.**

Matt. 10:16. I am sending you out like sheep among wolves. Therefore be as shrewd as snakes and as innocent as doves.

6. **If you are falsely accused, trust God to lead you.**

Matt. 10:17–20. Be on your guard against men; they will hand you over to the local councils and flog you in their synagogues. On my account you will be brought before governors and kings as witnesses to them and to the Gentiles. But when they arrest you, do not worry about what to say or how to say it. At that time you will be given what to say, for it will not be you speaking, but the Spirit of your Father speaking through you.

7. **One need not get depressed due to severe persecution. Paul testifies to that.**

2 Cor. 4:8–9. We are hard pressed on every side, but not crushed; perplexed, but not in despair; persecuted, but not abandoned; struck down, but not destroyed.

2 Cor. 11:23–29. *(Paul tells of the many things he suffered at the hands of his persecutors.)*

8. **Those who suffer for the sake of Christ will be blessed and should count it an honor to do so.**

1 Peter 4:12–16. Dear friends, do not be surprised at the painful trial you are suffering, as though something strange were happening to you. But rejoice that you participate in the sufferings of Christ, so that you may be overjoyed when his glory is revealed. If you are insulted because of the name of Christ, you are blessed, for the Spirit of glory and of God rests on you. If you suffer, it should not be as a murderer or thief or any other kind of criminal, or even as a meddler. However, if you suffer as a Christian, do not be ashamed, but praise God that you bear that name.

9. **Never be ashamed to be identified with those who are being persecuted. Rather, suffer with them, if need be.**

2 Tim. 1:8–9. Do not be ashamed to testify about our Lord, or ashamed of me his prisoner. But join with me in suffering for the gospel, by the power of God, who has saved us and called us to a holy life—not because of anything we have done but because of his own purpose and grace.

10. **Do not be ashamed of the gospel. Testify boldly and be ready to suffer persecution.**

2 Tim. 2:3. Endure hardship with us like a good soldier of Christ Jesus.

2 Tim. 2:8–10. Remember Jesus Christ, raised from the dead, descended from David. This is my gospel, for which I am suffering even to the point of being chained like a criminal. But God's

word is not chained. Therefore I endure everything for the sake of the elect, that they too may obtain the salvation that is in Christ Jesus, with eternal glory.

11. **Do not be unsettled or let the devil lead you away from the faith through persecution.**

    1 Thess. 3:2–4. We sent Timothy, who is our brother and God's fellow worker in spreading the gospel of Christ, to strengthen and encourage you in your faith, so that no one would be unsettled by these trials. You know quite well that we were destined for them. In fact, when we were with you, we kept telling you that we would be persecuted.

12. **Jesus says that some do fall away when they are persecuted.**

    Matt. 13:1–9. *(the parable of the sower)*
    Matt. 13:18–23. *(Jesus interprets the parable.)*
    Matt. 13:20–21. What was sown on rocky places is the man who hears the word and at once receives it with joy. But since he has no root, he lasts only a short time. When trouble or persecution comes because of the word, he quickly falls away.

13. **Some compromise the gospel to avoid persecution. Don't be like that.**

    Gal. 6:12. Those who want to make a good impression outwardly are trying to compel you to be circumcised. The only reason they do this is to avoid being persecuted for the cross of Christ.

14. **Believers can keep God's Word when they are persecuted. David did.**

    Ps. 119:51. The arrogant mock me without restraint, but I do not turn from your law.
    Ps. 119:61. Though the wicked bind me with ropes, I will not forget your law.
    Ps. 119:69. Though the arrogant have smeared me with lies, I keep your precepts with all my heart.

15. **If persecutors threaten you, obey God rather than man, as did Peter and John.**

    Acts 4:18–20. Then they called them in again and commanded them not to speak or teach at all in the name of Jesus. But Peter and John replied, "Judge for yourselves whether it is right in God's sight to obey you rather than God. For we cannot help speaking about what we have seen and heard."

Acts 5:17–32. *(The apostles went on preaching the gospel.)*

Acts 5:29. Peter and the other apostles replied: "We must obey God rather than men!"

Acts 5:41–42. The apostles left the Sanhedrin, rejoicing because they had been counted worthy of suffering disgrace for the Name. Day after day, in the temple courts and from house to house, they never stopped teaching and proclaiming the good news that Jesus is the Christ.

16. Paul and Silas sang hymns while they were imprisoned.

Acts 16:25. About midnight Paul and Silas were praying and singing hymns to God, and the other prisoners were listening to them.

17. Paul was willing to die for the sake of Christ.

Acts 21:12–13. When we heard this, we and the people there pleaded with Paul not to go up to Jerusalem. Then Paul answered, "Why are you weeping and breaking my heart? I am ready not only to be bound, but also to die in Jerusalem for the name of the Lord Jesus."

18. Those who are persecuted for righteousness' sake will be blessed.

Matt. 5:10–12. Blessed are those who are persecuted because of righteousness, for theirs is the kingdom of heaven. Blessed are you when people insult you, persecute you and falsely say all kinds of evil against you because of me. Rejoice and be glad, because great is your reward in heaven, for in the same way they persecuted the prophets who were before you.

2 Tim. 4:6–8. I am already being poured out like a drink offering, and the time has come for my departure. I have fought the good fight, I have finished the race, I have kept the faith. Now there is in store for me the crown of righteousness, which the Lord, the righteous Judge, will award to me on that day—and not only to me, but also to all who have longed for his appearing.

Rev. 2:9–10. I know your afflictions and your poverty—yet you are rich! I know the slander of those who say they are Jews and are not, but are a synagogue of Satan. Do not be afraid of what you are about to suffer. I tell you, the devil will put some of you in prison to test you, and you will suffer persecution for ten days. Be faithful, even to the point of death, and I will give you the crown of life.

19. Hebrew Christians stood their ground under persecution and were rewarded for it.

Heb. 10:32–39.

Heb. 10:33–35. Sometimes you were publicly exposed to insult and persecution; at other times you stood side by side with those who were so treated. You sympathized with those in prison and joyfully accepted the confiscation of your property, because you knew that you yourselves had better and lasting possessions. So do not throw away your confidence; it will be richly rewarded.

20. Be willing to suffer even for doing good.

1 Peter 3:13–22.

1 Peter 3:13–14. Who is going to harm you if you are eager to do good? But even if you should suffer for what is right, you are blessed. "Do not fear what they fear; do not be frightened."

1 Peter 3:17. It is better, if it is God's will, to suffer for doing good than for doing evil.

21. Unconverted sinners will at times heap abuse on you because you no longer join them in their sin.

1 Peter 4:3–5. You have spent enough time in the past doing what pagans choose to do—living in debauchery, lust, drunkenness, orgies, carousing and detestable idolatry. They think it strange that you do not plunge with them into the same flood of dissipation, and they heap abuse on you. But they will have to give account to him who is ready to judge the living and the dead.

22. We who are saved by grace and through faith in Christ must also be willing and prepared to suffer for him.

Phil. 1:27–30.

Phil. 1:29–30. For it has been granted to you on behalf of Christ not only to believe on him, but also to suffer for him, since you are going through the same struggle you saw I had, and now hear I still have.

23. How should you react when you are persecuted? See how Paul handled it.

1 Cor. 4:9–13.

1 Cor. 4:11–13. To this very hour we go hungry and thirsty, we are in rags, we are brutally treated, we are homeless. We work hard with our own hands. When we are cursed, we bless; when we are persecuted, we endure it; when we are slandered, we answer kindly. Up to this moment we have become the scum of the earth, the refuse of the world.

Prayer, Waiting on the Lord

See also Trust, p. 186.

1. **The Lord's Prayer is our model.**
   Matt. 6:9–13.

2. **Pray "Our Father."**
   Matt. 6:9. This is how you should pray: "Our Father in heaven."

3. **Pray for daily needs.**
   Matt. 6:11. Give us today our daily bread.

4. **Pray daily for the forgiveness of sins.**
   Matt. 6:12. Forgive us our debts, as we also have forgiven our debtors.

5. **We can approach God boldly through Jesus, our high priest, who understands our needs.**
   Heb. 4:14–16. Since we have a great high priest who has gone through the heavens, Jesus the Son of God, let us hold firmly to the faith we profess. For we do not have a high priest who is unable to sympathize with our weaknesses, but we have one who has been tempted in every way, just as we are—yet was without sin. Let us then approach the throne of grace with confidence, so that we may receive mercy and find grace to help us in our time of need.

6. **Cast all your anxiety on the Lord.**
   1 Peter 5:6–7. Humble yourselves, therefore, under God's mighty hand, that he may lift you up in due time. Cast all your anxiety on him because he cares for you.

7. Pray about everything instead of worrying.

    Phil. 4:6–7. Do not be anxious about anything, but in everything, by prayer and petition, with thanksgiving, present your requests to God. And the peace of God, which transcends all understanding, will guard your hearts and your minds in Christ Jesus.

8. Pray continually and give thanks in all circumstances.

    1 Thess. 5:17–18. Pray continually; give thanks in all circumstances, for this is God's will for you in Christ Jesus.

9. Pray in faith.

    James 1:6. When [anyone] asks [for wisdom], he must believe and not doubt, because he who doubts is like a wave of the sea, blown and tossed by the wind.

10. In time of sickness, pray.

    James 5:14–16.

11. The prayer of a righteous person is powerful.

    James 5:16. Confess your sins to each other and pray for each other so that you may be healed. The prayer of a righteous man is powerful and effective.

12. Dare to pray for great things, as did Elijah.

    James 5:17–18. Elijah was a man just like us. He prayed earnestly that it would not rain, and it did not rain on the land for three and a half years. Again he prayed, and the heavens gave rain, and the earth produced its crops.

13. God hears and answers prayer; he is near to his children.

    Ps. 34:15–18. The eyes of the LORD are on the righteous and his ears are attentive to their cry; the face of the LORD is against those who do evil, to cut off the memory of them from the earth. The righteous cry out, and the LORD hears them; he delivers them from all their troubles. The LORD is close to the brokenhearted and saves those who are crushed in spirit.

14. Pray and work, using the means available to you.

    Neh. 4:9. We prayed to our God and posted a guard day and night to meet this threat.

15. **In all your ways acknowledge the Lord.**

    Prov. 3:5–6. Trust in the LORD with all your heart and lean not on your own understanding; in all your ways acknowledge him, and he will make your paths straight.

16. **Seek the Lord while he may be found.**

    Isa. 55:6. Seek the LORD while he may be found; call on him while he is near.

17. **Thank God for his grace and mercy, praise him, and keep seeking his mercy.**

    Ps. 105:1–4.

18. **Praise and thank God for answered prayer.**

    Ps. 66:13–20.

    Ps. 66:17–20. I cried out to him with my mouth; his praise was on my tongue. If I had cherished sin in my heart, the LORD would not have listened; but God has surely listened and heard my voice in prayer. Praise be to God, who has not rejected my prayer or withheld his love from me!

19. **Pray for the forgiveness of sins.**

    Pss. 32 and 51.

    Jer. 29:12–13. Then you will call upon me and come and pray to me, and I will listen to you. You will seek me and find me when you seek me with all your heart.

    Matt. 11:28–30. Come to me, all you who are weary and burdened, and I will give you rest. Take my yoke upon you and learn from me, for I am gentle and humble in heart, and you will find rest for your souls. For my yoke is easy and my burden is light.

    Rom. 10:13. Everyone who calls on the name of the Lord will be saved.

    1 John 1:7–9.

    See also Forgiveness of Sins, p. 72.

20. **Call on the Lord in time of trouble.**

    Ps. 50:15. Call upon me in the day of trouble; I will deliver you, and you will honor me.

21. **Because Jesus was tried, as we are, he is able to help us.**

    Heb. 2:18. Because he himself suffered when he was tempted, he is able to help those who are being tempted.

Heb. 3:1. Therefore, holy brothers, who share in the heavenly calling, fix your thoughts on Jesus, the apostle and high priest whom we confess.

22. God answers intercessory prayer.

Acts 12:1–17. *(Peter was unjustly imprisoned. The church met for prayer. Peter was soon set free.)*

Acts 12:5. Peter was kept in prison, but the church was earnestly praying to God for him.

Acts 12:12. When [he realized that the angel had rescued him from prison], he went to the house of Mary the mother of John, also called Mark, where many people had gathered and were praying.

Progressive Sanctification
(Growing in Faith and Godliness)

See also Overcoming Sin, p. 117.

1. **Keep growing in the grace and knowledge of Jesus Christ.**

    2 Peter 3:18. But grow in the grace and knowledge of our Lord and Savior Jesus Christ. To him be glory both now and forever! Amen.

2. **Do not be content to be an immature Christian, as was the case with many Hebrew believers.**

    Heb. 5:11–6:4.

    Heb. 5:12–14. In fact, though by this time you ought to be teachers, you need someone to teach you the elementary truths of God's word all over again. You need milk, not solid food! Anyone who lives on milk, being still an infant, is not acquainted with the teaching about righteousness. But solid food is for the mature, who by constant use have trained themselves to distinguish good from evil.

3. **God works in us through his word to bring us to spiritual maturity, to sanctify us.**

    John 17:17. *(Jesus, thinking of his redeemed people, prayed)* Sanctify them by the truth; your word is truth.

    Col. 3:16. Let the word of Christ dwell in you richly as you teach and admonish one another with all wisdom, and as you sing psalms, hymns and spiritual songs with gratitude in your hearts to God.

1 Peter 2:2–3. Like newborn babies, crave pure spiritual milk, so that by it you may grow up in your salvation, now that you have tasted that the Lord is good.

Ps. 119:11. I have hidden your word in my heart that I might not sin against you.

Ps. 119:105. Your word is a lamp to my feet and a light for my path.

4. **The Bible, the inspired, inerrant word of God is that by which he trains us in righteousness so that we may be thoroughly equipped for every good work.**

   2 Tim. 3:16–17. All scripture is God-breathed and useful for teaching, rebuking, correcting and training in righteousness, so that the man of God may be thoroughly equipped for every good work.

5. **The Counselor, the Holy Spirit, teaches us through his own word.**

   John 14:25–26. All this I have spoken while still with you. But the Counselor, the Holy Spirit, whom the Father will send in my name, will teach you all things and will remind you of everything I have said to you.

6. **The word of God is immeasurably effective.**

   Heb. 4:12. For the word of God is living and active. Sharper than any double-edged sword, it penetrates even to dividing soul and spirit, joints and marrow; it judges the thoughts and attitudes of the heart.

7. **Like a runner in a race, keep pressing on until you have gained the victory, as did the apostle Paul.**

   Phil. 3:12–14. Not that I have already obtained all this, or have already been made perfect, but I press on to take hold of that for which Christ Jesus took hold of me. Brothers, I do not consider myself to have taken hold of it. But one thing I do: Forgetting what is behind me and straining toward what is ahead, I press on toward the goal to win the prize for which God has called me heavenward in Christ Jesus.

   Note: Paul had a healthy dissatisfaction with himself, although he was already a mature Christian. He would neither focus on past failure, nor would he allow himself to become discouraged after he did fall. He kept pressing on.

8. **Get rid of everything that might hinder you and run the race with perseverance.**

    Heb. 12:1. Therefore, since we are surrounded by such a great cloud of witnesses, let us throw off everything that hinders and the sin that so easily entangles, and let us run with perseverance the race marked out for us.

9. **Fix your eyes on Jesus, the author and perfecter of your faith. Focus on all he did to save you!**

    Heb. 12:2. Let us fix our eyes on Jesus, the author and perfecter of our faith, who for the joy set before him endured the cross, scorning its shame, and sat down at the right hand of the throne of God.

10. **Train yourself to be godly. Be like an athlete, who persists in training. That's what Paul counseled Timothy to do.**

    1 Tim. 4:7–8. Have nothing to do with the godless myths and old wives' tales; rather, train yourself to be godly. For physical training is of some value, but godliness has value for all things, holding promise for both the present life and the life to come.

11. **Put much effort into living a godly life.**

    2 Peter 3:14. So then, dear friends, since you are looking forward to this, make every effort to be found spotless, blameless and at peace with him.

12. **Abide in Jesus Christ, the vine, through whom alone you can bear much fruit, to glorify God.**

    John 15:1–8.

    John 15:1. I am the true vine, and my Father is the gardener.

    John 15:5. I am the vine; you are the branches. If a man remains in me and I in him, he will bear much fruit; apart from me you can do nothing.

    John 15:8. This is to my Father's glory, that you bear much fruit, showing yourselves to be my disciples.

13. **Imitate Jesus so that you will become more and more Christ-like.**

    1 John 2:6. Whoever claims to live in him must walk as Jesus did.

    For more on this see Imitating Jesus, p. 93.

14. **The apostle Peter lists some Christ-like virtues we should seek after.**

    2 Peter 1:5–9.

    2 Peter 1:5–7. For this very reason, make every effort to add to your faith goodness; and to goodness, knowledge; and to knowledge, self-control; and to self-control, perseverance; and to perseverance, godliness; and to godliness, brotherly kindness; and to brotherly kindness, love.

15. **We must be motivated to work at growing in faith and godliness by the victory we have through the suffering, death and resurrection of Jesus Christ.**

    1 Cor. 15:57–58. But thanks be to God! He gives us the victory through our Lord Jesus Christ. Therefore, my dear brothers, stand firm. Let nothing move you. Always give yourselves fully to the work of the Lord, because you know that your labor in the Lord is not in vain.

    2 Cor. 7:1. Since we have these promises, dear friends, let us purify ourselves from everything that contaminates body and spirit, perfecting holiness out of reverence for God.

    Rom. 12:1–2. Therefore I urge you, brothers, in view of God's mercy (in giving you salvation) to offer your bodies as living sacrifices, holy and pleasing to God—this is your spiritual act of worship. Do not conform any longer to the pattern of this world, but be transformed by the renewing of your mind. Then you will be able to test and approve what God's will is—his good, pleasing and perfect will.

16. **God uses his word to revive the soul, make wise the simple, give joy to the heart, give light to the eyes, and much more.**

    Ps. 19:7–11.

    Ps. 19:7–8. The law of the LORD is perfect, reviving the soul. The statutes of the LORD are trustworthy, making wise the simple. The precepts of the LORD are right, giving joy to the heart. The commands of the LORD are radiant, giving light to the eyes.

17. **The Lord requires us to keep working out our salvation in every area of life, since he works in us by his word and spirit.**

    Phil. 2:12–13. Continue to work out your salvation with fear and trembling, for it is God who works in you to will and to act according to his good purpose.

18. **God is graciously transforming every Christian more and more into the likeness of Jesus Christ.**

2 Cor. 3:18. And we, who with unveiled faces all reflect the Lord's glory, are being transformed into his likeness with ever-increasing glory, which comes from the Lord, who is the Spirit.

Providence of God

See also Comfort, p. 37; and Trust, p. 186.

1. **God sovereignly works all things according to his will.**

   Eph. 1:11. In him we were also chosen, having been predestined according to the plan of him who works out everything in conformity with the purpose of his will.

2. **God's sovereign rule extends over all things.**

   Ps. 103:19. The LORD has established his throne in heaven, and his kingdom rules over all.

   Acts 17:28. "In him we live and move and have our being." As some of your own poets have said, "We are his offspring."

   Rom. 11:36. From him and through him and to him are all things. To him be the glory forever! Amen.

3. **God cares for the birds and the flowers and certainly will, then, care for his children.**

   Matt. 6:25–34.

   Matt. 6:26. Look at the birds of the air; they do not sow or reap or store away in barns, and yet your heavenly Father feeds them. Are you not much more valuable than they?

   Matt. 6:30. If that is how God clothes the grass of the field, which is here today and tomorrow is thrown into the fire, will he not much more clothe you, O you of little faith?

4. **God controls all the forces of nature and provides for all his creatures, especially his children.**

   Ps. 104; Ps. 145; Ps. 147.

5. God used ravens to care for Elijah.

1 Kings 17:1–6.

1 Kings 17:4–5. "You will drink from the brook, and I have ordered the ravens to feed you there." So he did what the LORD had told him. He went to the Kerith Ravine, east of the Jordan, and stayed there. The ravens brought him bread and meat in the morning and bread and meat in the evening, and he drank from the brook.

6. By sending his people manna from heaven each day, God revealed his faithfulness, power, and love.

Exod. 16.

7. God is the potter, we are the clay. Be submissive to him.

Jer. 18:1–10.

Jer. 18:5–6. Then the word of the LORD came to me: "O house of Israel, can I not do with you as this potter does?" declares the LORD. "Like clay in the hand of the potter, so are you in my hand, O house of Israel."

Isa. 45:9–13.

Isa. 45:9–11. Woe to him who quarrels with his Maker, to him who is but a potsherd among the potsherds on the ground. Does the clay say to the potter, "What are you making?" Does your work say, "He has no hands"? Woe to him who says to his father, "What have you begotten?" or to his mother, "What have you brought to birth?" This is what the LORD says—the Holy One of Israel, and its Maker: Concerning things to come, do you question me about my children, or give me orders about the work of my hands?

8. God uses wicked rulers to fulfill his purposes for his children.

Isa. 45:12–13. It is I who made the earth and created mankind upon it. My own hands stretched out the heavens; I marshaled their starry hosts. I will raise up Cyrus in my righteousness: I will make all his ways straight. He will rebuild my city and set my exiles free, but not for a price or reward, says the LORD Almighty.

Ezra 7:1–10. *(God moved King Artaxerxes to give Ezra what he asked for, because "the hand of the LORD his God was on him.")*

Ezra 7:6. This Ezra came up from Babylon. He was a teacher well versed in the Law of Moses, which the LORD, the God of Israel, had given. The king had granted him everything he asked, for the hand of the LORD his God was on him.

Ezra 7:10. Ezra had devoted himself to the study and observance of the Law of the LORD, and to teaching its decrees and laws in Israel.

9. **God blesses those who by faith take refuge in him.**

Ruth. *(The whole Book of Ruth reveals this very beautifully.)*

Ruth 2:12. Boaz replied, ". . . May the LORD repay you for what you have done. May you be richly rewarded by the LORD, the God of Israel, under whose wings you have come to take refuge."

Ruth 2:20. *(After Ruth had gleaned in Boaz's field, Naomi praised him.)* "The LORD bless him!" Naomi said to her daughter-in-law. "The LORD has not stopped showing his kindness to the living and the dead." She added, "That man is our close relative; he is one of our kinsman-redeemers."

10. **Not one of God's promises goes unfulfilled.**

Josh. 23:14. Now I am about to go the way of all the earth. You know with all your heart and soul that not one of all the good promises the LORD your God gave you has failed. Every promise has been fulfilled; not one has failed.

11. **God will also carry out his threats.**

Josh. 23:15–16. But just as every good promise of the LORD your God has come true, so the LORD will bring on you all the evil he has threatened, until he has destroyed you from this good land he has given you. If you violate the covenant of the LORD your God, which he commanded you, and go and serve other gods and bow down to them, the LORD's anger will burn against you, and you will quickly perish from the good land he has given you.

12. **God used Gideon's small band to defeat Israel's enemies.**

Judg. 7:1–25.

Judg. 7:2–3. The LORD said to Gideon, "You have too many men for me to deliver Midian into their hands. In order that Israel may not boast against me that her own strength has saved her, announce now to the people, 'Anyone who trembles with fear may turn back and leave Mount Gilead.'" So twenty-two thousand men left, while ten thousand remained.

13. **God promises to go with those to whom he gives a difficult task.**

Deut. 31:7–8. Then Moses summoned Joshua and said to him in the presence of all Israel, "Be strong and courageous, for you must go with this people into the land that the LORD swore to their forefathers to give them, and you must divide it among them as their inheritance. The LORD himself goes before you and will be with you; he will never leave you nor forsake you. Do not be afraid; do not be discouraged."

14. Joseph acknowledged God's providence in being sold into slavery.

Gen. 45:1–14. *(Joseph made himself known to his brothers.)*

Gen. 45:4–8. Then Joseph said to his brothers, "Come close to me." When they had done so, he said, "I am your brother Joseph, the one you sold into Egypt! And now, do not be distressed and do not be angry with yourselves for selling me here, because it was to save lives that God sent me ahead of you. For two years now there has been famine in the land, and for the next five years there will not be plowing and reaping. But God sent me ahead of you to preserve for you a remnant on earth and to save your lives by a great deliverance. So then, it was not you who sent me here, but God. He made me father to Pharaoh, lord of his entire household and ruler of all Egypt."

Gen. 50:15–21. *(Joseph reassured his brothers of his forgiveness toward them.)*

Gen. 50:19–21. Joseph said to them, "Don't be afraid. Am I in the place of God? You intended to harm me, but God intended it for good to accomplish what is now being done, the saving of many lives. So then, don't be afraid. I will provide for you and your children." And he reassured them and spoke kindly to them.

15. The Lord brings grief at times, but he also shows mercy.

Lam. 3:31–33. Men are not cast off by the LORD forever. Though he brings grief, he will show compassion, so great is his unfailing love. For he does not willingly bring affliction or grief to the children of men.

16. God decrees and brings both hardship and good times.

Lam. 3:37–42. Who can speak and have it happen if the LORD has not decreed it? Is it not from the mouth of the Most High that both calamities and good things come? Why should any living man complain when punished for his sins? Let us examine our ways and test them, and let us return to the LORD. Let us lift up our hearts

149

and our hands to God in heaven, and say: "We have sinned and rebelled and you have not forgiven."

17. **God faithfully cares for us as a shepherd cares for his sheep.**

Ps. 23.

18. **When we please the Lord, he makes even our enemies to be at peace with us.**

Prov. 16:7. When a man's ways are pleasing to the LORD, he makes even his enemies live at peace with him.

19. **All rulers are under God's control.**

Prov. 21:1. The king's heart is in the hand of the LORD; he directs it like a watercourse wherever he pleases.

20. **God has sovereignly planned what shall come to pass and he sovereignly carries out his plans.**

Isa. 46:10–13.

Isa. 46:10. I make known the end from the beginning, from ancient times, what is still to come. I say: My purpose will stand, and I will do all that I please.

21. **It is God who gives rain. Pray for rain in time of need.**

Zech. 10:1. Ask the LORD for rain in the springtime; it is the LORD who makes the storm clouds. He gives showers of rain to men, and plants of the field to everyone.

22. **The story of Jonah strikingly reveals God's providence.**

Jonah 1:4. Then the LORD sent a great wind on the sea, and such a violent storm arose that the ship threatened to break up.

Jonah 1:17. But the LORD provided a great fish to swallow Jonah, and Jonah was inside the fish three days and three nights.

Jonah 2:10. And the LORD commanded the fish, and it vomited Jonah onto dry land.

Jonah 4:6–8. Then the LORD God provided a vine and made it grow up over Jonah to give shade for his head to ease his discomfort, and Jonah was very happy about the vine. But at dawn the next day God provided a worm, which chewed the vine so that it withered. When the sun rose, God provided a scorching east wind, and the sun blazed on Jonah's head so that he grew faint. He wanted to die, and said, "It would be better for me to die than to live."

23. God chose Jeremiah to be a prophet even before he was born.

Jer. 1:4–5. The word of the LORD came to me, saying, "Before I formed you in the womb I knew you, before you were born I set you apart; I appointed you as a prophet to the nations."

24. God sovereignly works out his plans, his perfect will. No one can hinder or stop him.

Prov. 16:4. The LORD works out everything for his own ends— even the wicked for a day of disaster.

Prov. 16:9. In his heart a man plans his course, but the LORD determines his steps.

Prov. 16:33. The lot is cast into the lap, but its every decision is from the LORD.

Prov. 21:30. There is no wisdom, no insight, no plan that can succeed against the LORD.

Ps. 135:6. The LORD does whatever pleases him, in the heavens and on the earth, in the seas and all their depths.

25. God sovereignly used Paul's imprisonment in Rome to advance the gospel.

Phil. 1:12–14. Now I want you to know, brothers, that what has happened to me has really served to advance the gospel. As a result, it has become clear throughout the whole palace guard and to everyone else that I am in chains for Christ. Because of my chains, most of the brothers in the Lord have been encouraged to speak the word of God more courageously and fearlessly.

26. God prepared Joseph to become governor over Egypt. Such acts of God reveal his personal involvement in the lives of his children.

Acts 7:9–10. Because the patriarchs were jealous of Joseph, they sold him as a slave into Egypt. But God was with him and rescued him from all his troubles. He gave Joseph wisdom and enabled him to gain the goodwill of Pharaoh king of Egypt; so he made him ruler over Egypt and all his palace.

27. God kept Moses alive and ordained that he should be educated in all the wisdom of Egypt so that he could lead the children of Israel.

Acts 7:20–22. At that time Moses was born, and he was no ordinary child. For three months he was cared for in his father's house.

When he was placed outside, Pharaoh's daughter took him and brought him up as her own son. Moses was educated in all the wisdom of the Egyptians and was powerful in speech and action.

28. **God gave Daniel and his three friends special intellectual ability and wisdom to fulfill his purposes. See how God works for his children.**

    Dan. 1:17. To these four young men God gave knowledge and understanding of all kinds of literature and learning. And Daniel could understand visions and dreams of all kinds.

    Dan. 6:3. Now Daniel so distinguished himself among the administrators and the satraps by his exceptional qualities that the king planned to set him over the whole kingdom.

29. **God put it into the heart of the evil king, Cyrus, to allow his people to return to the promised land.**

    Ezra 1:1. In the first year of Cyrus king of Persia, in order to fulfill the word of the LORD spoken by Jeremiah, the LORD moved the heart of Cyrus king of Persia to make a proclamation throughout his realm and to put it in writing.

30. **The hand of God was on Nehemiah, that's why King Artaxerses granted his requests.**

    Neh. 2:4–9.

    Neh. 2:8. "And may I have a letter to Asaph, keeper of the king's forest, so he will give me the timber to make beams for the gates of the citadel by the temple and for the city wall and for the residence I will occupy?" And because the gracious hand of my God was upon me, the king granted my requests.

Repentance

See also Progressive Sanctification, p. 141; Overcoming Sin, p. 117; and Warnings, p. 192.

1. Jesus calls sinners to repentance.

Luke 5:27–32. *(The Pharisees objected that Jesus ate with tax collectors and sinners. Jesus explained exactly why he did this.)*

Luke 5:31–32. Jesus answered them, "It is not the healthy who need a doctor, but the sick. I have not come to call the righteous, but sinners to repentance."

2. Jesus calls needy sinners to repentance that leads to salvation.

Matt. 4:17. From that time on Jesus began to preach, "Repent, for the kingdom of heaven is near."

3. Repentance must be from the heart, genuine.

Mark 7:20–23. He went on: "What comes out of a man is what makes him 'unclean.' For from within, out of men's hearts, come evil thoughts, sexual immorality, theft, murder, adultery, greed, malice, deceit, lewdness, envy, slander, arrogance and folly. All these evils come from inside and make a man 'unclean.'"

Jer. 4:3–4. This is what the LORD says to the men of Judah and to Jerusalem: "Break up your unplowed ground and do not sow among thorns. Circumcise yourselves to the LORD, circumcise your hearts, you men of Judah and people of Jerusalem, or my wrath will break out and burn like fire because of the evil you have done— burn with no one to quench it."

Joel 2:12–13. "Even now," declares the LORD, "return to me with all your heart, with fasting and weeping and mourning." Rend your heart and not your garments. Return to the LORD your God, for he is gracious and compassionate, slow to anger and abounding in love, and he relents from sending calamity.

4. Godly sorrow brings repentance that leads to salvation.

2 Cor. 7:8–11. *(Motivated by love, Paul led the Corinthian Christians to a godly sorrow, which brought repentance and salvation.)*

2 Cor. 7:10–11. Godly sorrow brings repentance that leads to salvation and leaves no regret, but worldly sorrow brings death. See what this godly sorrow has produced in you: what earnestness, what eagerness to clear yourselves, what indignation, what alarm, what longing, what concern, what readiness to see justice done. At every point you have proved yourselves to be innocent in this matter.

5. There is joy in heaven over one sinner who repents.

Luke 15. *(Jesus taught this in the parables of the lost sheep, the lost coin, and the lost son.)*

Luke 15:7. I tell you that in the same way there will be more rejoicing in heaven over one sinner who repents than over ninety-nine righteous persons who do not need to repent.

6. God calls sinners to seek him, to forsake their evil ways, and promises to forgive them.

Isa. 55:6–7. Seek the LORD while he may be found; call on him while he is near. Let the wicked forsake his way and the evil man his thoughts. Let him turn to the LORD, and he will have mercy on him, and to our God, for he will freely pardon.

7. God calls to repentance those who have set up idols in their hearts and practice evil.

Ezek. 14:1–11.

Ezek. 14:6. Therefore say to the house of Israel, "This is what the Sovereign LORD says: Repent! Turn from your idols and renounce all your detestable practices!"

8. When a wayward sinner repents and turns back to God, he will live.

Ezek. 18:21–22. If a wicked man turns away from all the sins he has committed and keeps all my decrees and does what is just and right, he will surely live; he will not die. None of the offenses he has committed will be remembered against him. Because of the righteous things he has done, he will live.

9. God takes no pleasure in the death of the wicked.

Ezek. 18:23. Do I take any pleasure in the death of the wicked? declares the Sovereign LORD. Rather, am I not pleased when they turn from their ways and live?

10. The Lord urgently calls sinners to turn from their evil ways.

Ezek. 18:30–32. Therefore, O house of Israel, I will judge you, each one according to his ways, declares the Sovereign LORD. Repent! Turn away from all your offenses; then sin will not be your downfall. Rid yourselves of all the offenses you have committed, and get a new heart and a new spirit. Why will you die, O house of Israel? For I take no pleasure in the death of anyone, declares the Sovereign LORD. Repent and live!

11. Jesus pronounced his judgment on those who refused to repent.

Matt. 11:20–24. Then Jesus began to denounce the cities in which most of his miracles had been performed, because they did not repent. "Woe to you, Korazin! Woe to you, Bethsaida! If the miracles that were performed in you had been performed in Tyre and Sidon, they would have repented long ago in sackcloth and ashes. But I tell you, it will be more bearable for Tyre and Sidon on the day of judgment than for you. And you, Capernaum, will you be lifted up to the skies? No, you will go down to the depths. If the miracles that were performed in you had been performed in Sodom, it would have remained to this day. But I tell you that it will be more bearable for Sodom on the day of judgment than for you."

12. Out of his kindness, God keeps calling sinners to repentance.

Rom. 2:4. Do you show contempt for the riches of his kindness, tolerance and patience, not realizing that God's kindness leads you toward repentance?

13. If you stubbornly refuse to repent, God will punish you. If you do repent, he will forgive you and grant you eternal life.

Rom. 2:5–11.

Rom. 2:5–6. Because of your stubbornness and your unrepentant heart, you are storing up wrath against yourself for the day of God's wrath, when his righteous judgment will be revealed. God "will give to each person according to what he has done."

14. **Calamity comes to those who do not give heed to God's call to repentance.**

     Prov. 1:24–33.

     Prov. 1:24–28. Since you rejected me when I called and no one gave heed when I stretched out my hand, since you ignored all my advice and would not accept my rebuke, I in turn will laugh at your disaster; I will mock when calamity overtakes you—when calamity overtakes you like a storm, when disaster sweeps over you like a whirlwind, when distress and troubles overwhelm you. Then they will call to me but I will not answer; they will look for me but will not find me.

15. **An adulterous woman repented and turned to Christ and was forgiven.**

     Luke 7:36–50.

     Luke 7:37–38. When a woman who had lived a sinful life in that town learned that Jesus was eating at the Pharisee's house, she brought an alabaster jar of perfume, and as she stood behind him at his feet weeping, she began to wet his feet with her tears. Then she wiped them with her hair, kissed them and poured perfume on them.

     Luke 7:48–50. Then Jesus said to her, "Your sins are forgiven." The other guests began to say among themselves, "Who is this who even forgives sins?" Jesus said to the woman, "Your faith has saved you; go in peace."

16. **God poured out his anger on unrepentant Israelites.**

     Isa. 42:23–25. Which of you will listen to this or pay close attention in time to come? Who handed Jacob over to become loot, and Israel to the plunderers? Was it not the LORD, against whom we have sinned? For they would not follow his ways; they did not obey his law. So he poured out on them his burning anger, the violence of war. It enveloped them in flames, yet they did not understand; it consumed them, but they did not take it to heart.

17. **Return to the Lord and he will return to you.**

     Mal. 3:7. "Return to me, and I will return to you," says the LORD Almighty.

18. **Those who mourn on account of their sin are blessed.**

     Matt. 5:4. Blessed are those who mourn, for they will be comforted.

19. **If God's people turn from their wicked ways, he will forgive them.**

    2 Chron. 7:14. If my people, who are called by my name, will humble themselves and pray and seek my face and turn from their wicked ways, then will I hear from heaven and will forgive their sin and will heal their land.

20. **Paul preached that all sinners must repent, turn to God and prove their repentance by their deeds.**

    Acts 26:19–20. So then, King Agrippa, I was not disobedient to the vision from heaven. First to those in Damascus, then to those in Jerusalem and in all Judea, and to the Gentiles also, I preached that they should repent and turn to God and prove their repentance by their deeds.

Salvation
(Leading a Person to Christ)

Apart from Christ, we are helpless and sinful.

We are all sinners.

1. **We are all born in sin.**

    Ps. 51:5. Surely I have been a sinner from birth, sinful from the time my mother conceived me.

2. **We all, like sheep, have gone astray.**

    Isa. 53:6. We all, like sheep, have gone astray, each of us has turned to his own way; and the LORD has laid on him the iniquity of us all.

3. **All have sinned through Adam.**

    Rom. 5:12. Just as sin has entered the world through one man, and death through sin, and in this way death came to all men, because all sinned.

    Rom. 5:19. Just as through the disobedience of the one man the many were made sinners, so also through the obedience of the one man the many will be made righteous.

4. **Jews and Gentiles alike are sinners.**

    Rom. 3:9–12. What shall we conclude then? Are we any better? Not at all! We have already made the charge that Jews and Gentiles alike are all under sin. As it is written: "There is no one righteous, not even one; there is no one who understands, no one who seeks God. All have turned away, they have together become worthless; there is no one who does good, not even one.

    Rom. 3:22–24. There is no difference, for all have sinned and fall short of the glory of God.

5. **We are like lost sheep whom Jesus goes out to seek.**
   Luke 15:3–7.

6. **We are like the prodigal son.**
   Luke 15:11–24.

7. **Even our righteous acts are as filthy rags.**

   Isa. 64:6. All of us have become like one who is unclean, and all our righteous acts are like filthy rags; we all shrivel up like a leaf, and like the wind our sins sweep us away.

8. **If you claim to be without sin you deceive yourself and even make God out to be a liar.**

   1 John 1:8–10. If we claim to be without sin, we deceive ourselves and the truth is not in us. If we confess our sins, he is faithful and just and will forgive us our sins us and purify us from all unrighteousness. If we claim we have not sinned, we make him out to be a liar and his word has no place in our lives.

9. **Apart from God's grace, our hearts are deceitful, beyond cure.**

   Jer. 17:9. The heart is deceitful above all things and beyond cure. Who can understand it?

10. **In the light of God's holiness we see that we are very sinful. That is what happened to Isaiah.**

    Isa. 6:1–5. In the year that King Uzziah died, I saw the LORD seated on a throne, high and exalted, and the train of his robe filled the temple. Above him were seraphs, each with six wings: With two wings they covered their faces, with two they covered their feet, and with two they were flying. And they were calling to one another: "Holy, holy, holy is the LORD Almighty; the whole earth is full of his glory." At the sound of their voices the doorposts and thresholds shook and the temple was filled with smoke. "Woe to me!" I cried. "I am ruined! For I am a man of unclean lips, and I live among a people of unclean lips and my eyes have seen the King, the LORD Almighty."

We are in spiritual bondage.

1. **By nature all are in sin's bondage. Christ sets us free.**
   John 8:31–36.

John 8:34–36. I tell you the truth, everyone who sins is a slave to sin. Now a slave has no permanent place in the family, but a son belongs to it forever. So if the Son sets you free, you will be free indeed.

2. To continue to live in sin is bondage.

2 Peter 2:19. They [false prophets] promise . . . freedom, while they themselves are slaves of depravity—for a man is a slave to whatever has mastered him.

3. Jesus sets us free.

Rom. 6:16–18. Don't you know that when you offer yourselves to someone to obey him as slaves, you are slaves to the one whom you obey—whether you are slaves to sin, which leads to death, or to obedience, which leads to righteousness? But thanks be to God that, though you used to be slaves to sin, you wholeheartedly obeyed the form of teaching to which you were entrusted. You have been set free from sin and have become slaves to righteousness.

We are alienated from God.

1. Outside of Christ we are at odds with God.

Col. 1:21–22. Once you were alienated from God and were enemies in your minds because of your evil behavior. But now he has reconciled you by Christ's physical body through death to present you holy in his sight, without blemish and free from accusation.

2. Without Christ we are without hope.

Eph. 2:12–13. Remember that at that time [before salvation in Christ] you were separate from Christ, excluded from citizenship in Israel and foreigners to the covenants of the promise, without hope and without God in the world. But now in Christ Jesus you who once were far away have been brought near through the blood of Christ.

Knowledge of sin comes by the law of God.

1. Through knowledge of the law we become conscious of sin.

Rom. 3:20. No one will be declared righteous in his sight by observing the law; rather, through the law we become conscious of sin.

2. The law helps us understand sin.

Rom. 7:7. What shall we say, then? Is the law sin? Certainly not! Indeed I would not have known what sin was except through the law. For I would not have known what it was to covet if the law had not said, "Do not covet."

3. Jesus gave us his summary of the law.

Matt. 22:37–40. Jesus replied: "'Love the Lord your God with all your heart and with all your soul and with all your mind.' This is the first and greatest commandment. And the second is like it: 'Love your neighbor as yourself.' All the Law and the Prophets hang on these two commandments."

4. God has given us the Ten Commandments.

Exod. 20:1–17.

God in his justice punishes sinners.

1. God first revealed his justice to Adam.

Gen. 2:16–17. The LORD God commanded the man, "You are free to eat from any tree in the garden; but you must not eat from the tree of the knowledge of good and evil, for when you eat of it you will surely die."

2. The result of sin is death.

Rom. 5:12. Just as sin entered the world through one man, and death through sin, and in this way death came to all men, because all sinned.

Rom. 6:23. The wages of sin is death, but the gift of God is eternal life in Christ Jesus our Lord.

3. By nature we are all under the curse of God.

Gal. 3:10. All who rely on observing the law are under a curse, for it is written: "Cursed is everyone who does not continue to do everything written in the Book of the Law."

See also Warnings, p. 192.

We cannot save ourselves in any way.

1. By nature we are at enmity with God.

Rom. 8:7–8. The sinful mind is hostile to God. It does not submit to God's law, nor can it do so. Those controlled by the sinful nature cannot please God.

2. **By nature we are dead in sin and are objects of God's wrath.**

Eph. 2:1–5. As for you, you were dead in your transgressions and sins, in which you used to live when you followed the ways of this world and of the ruler of the kingdom of the air, the spirit who is now at work in those who are disobedient. All of us also lived among them at one time, gratifying the cravings of our sinful nature and following its desires and thoughts. Like the rest, we were by nature objects of wrath. But because of his great love for us, God, who is rich in mercy, made us alive with Christ even when we were dead in transgressions—it is by grace you have been saved.

3. **We are saved only by grace, through faith.**

Eph. 2:8–9. It is by grace you have been saved, through faith—and this not from yourselves, it is the gift of God—not by works, so that no one can boast.

4. **God saves us through a rebirth and renewal by the Holy Spirit.**

Titus 3:4–7. When the kindness and love of God our Savior appeared, he saved us, not because of righteous things we had done, but because of his mercy. He saved us through the washing of rebirth and renewal by the Holy Spirit, whom he poured out on us generously through Jesus Christ our Savior, so that, having been justified by his grace, we might become heirs having the hope of eternal life.

Jesus saves us by grace, through faith.

Jesus suffered and died for sinners; those who believe in him will be saved.

1. **Isaiah depicts the suffering servant of Jehovah.**

Isa. 53:1–11.

Isa. 53:4–6. Surely he took up our infirmities and carried our sorrows, yet we considered him stricken by God, smitten by him, and afflicted. But he was pierced for our transgressions, he was crushed for our iniquities; the punishment that brought us peace was upon him, and by his wounds we are healed. We all, like sheep, have gone astray, each of us has turned to his own way; and the LORD has laid on him the iniquity of us all.

2. **All who receive Christ by faith are saved.**

John 1:12. To all who received him, to those who believed in his name, he gave the right to become children of God.

3. **As was prophesied, God gave his only Son so that those who believe in him may have eternal life.**

John 3:14–16. Just as Moses lifted up the snake in the desert, so the Son of Man must be lifted up, that everyone who believes in him may have eternal life. For God so loved the world that he gave his one and only Son, that whoever believes in him shall not perish but have eternal life.

4. **Jesus died for his sheep.**

John 10:11, 14–15. I am the good shepherd. The good shepherd lays down his life for the sheep. . . . I am the good shepherd; I know my sheep and my sheep know me—just as the Father knows me and I know the Father—and I lay down my life for the sheep.

5. **His sheep hear Jesus' voice and follow him and receive eternal life.**

John 10:27–28. My sheep listen to my voice; I know them, and they follow me. I give them eternal life, and they shall never perish; no one can snatch them out of my hand.

6. **We are redeemed through the blood of Christ.**

1 Peter 1:18–19. You know that it was not with perishable things such as silver or gold that you were redeemed from the empty way of life handed down to you from your forefathers, but with the precious blood of Christ, a lamb without blemish or defect.

7. **Christ loved the church and gave himself for her.**

Eph. 5:25–27. Husbands, love your wives, just as Christ loved the church and gave himself up for her to make her holy, cleansing her by the washing with water through the word, and to present her to himself as a radiant church, without stain or wrinkle or any other blemish, but holy and blameless.

8. **Jesus is the only mediator.**

1 Tim. 2:5–6. There is one God and one mediator between God and men, the man Christ Jesus, who gave himself as a ransom for all men—the testimony given in its proper time.

9. **Christ died for undeserving sinners, for many gracious purposes.**

Rom. 5:8. God demonstrates his own love for us in this: While we were still sinners, Christ died for us.

Phil. 2:8. Being found in appearance as a man, he humbled himself and became obedient to death—even death on a cross!

2 Cor. 5:21. God made him who had no sin to be sin for us, so that in him we might become the righteousness of God.

John 1:29. The next day John saw Jesus coming toward him and said, "Look, the Lamb of God, who takes away the sin of the world!"

1 John 4:9–10. This is how God showed his love among us: He sent his one and only Son into the world that we might live through him. This is love: not that we loved God, but that he loved us and sent his Son as an atoning sacrifice for our sins.

Gal. 3:13. Christ redeemed us from the curse of the law by becoming a curse for us, for it is written: "Cursed is everyone who is hung on a tree."

1 Peter 2:24. He himself bore our sins in his body on the tree, so that we might die to sins and live for righteousness; by his wounds you have been healed.

1 Peter 3:18. Christ died for sins once for all, the righteous for the unrighteous, to bring you to God. He was put to death in the body but made alive by the Spirit.

Heb. 9:14. How much more, then, will the blood of Christ who through the eternal Spirit offered himself unblemished to God, cleanse our consciences from acts that lead to death, so that we may serve the living God!

10. **We are forgiven, justified, and cleared of all guilt and condemnation by faith in Jesus Christ.**

Rom. 3:21–24. Now a righteousness from God, apart from law, has been made known, to which the Law and the Prophets testify. This righteousness from God comes through faith in Jesus Christ to all who believe. There is no difference, for all have sinned and fall short of the glory of God, and are justified freely by his grace through the redemption that came by Christ Jesus.

Rom. 5:1. Since we have been justified through faith, we have peace with God through our Lord Jesus Christ.

Rom. 8:1. There is now no condemnation for those who are in Christ Jesus.

Rom. 10:9–13. If you confess with your mouth, "Jesus is Lord," and believe in your heart that God raised him from the dead, you will be saved. For it is with your heart that you believe and are justified, and it is with your mouth that you confess and are saved. As the Scripture says, "Everyone who trusts in him will never be put to shame." For there is no difference between Jew and Gentile—the same Lord is Lord of all and richly blesses all who call on him, for, "Everyone who calls on the name of the Lord will be saved."

See also Forgiveness of Sins, p. 72.

Examples of those saved by grace, through faith.

1. **Levi, the tax collector.**
   Luke 5:27–32.

2. **Zacchaeus, the tax collector.**
   Luke 19:9–10. Jesus said to him, "Today salvation has come to this house, because this man, too, is a son of Abraham. For the Son of Man came to seek and to save what was lost."

3. **The penitent woman who wept at Jesus' feet.**
   Luke 7:48, 50. Then Jesus said to her, "Your sins are forgiven. . . . Your faith has saved you; go in peace."

4. **Many notorious sinners represented in Jesus' parables.**
   Luke 15:1–2. Now the tax collectors and "sinners" were all gathering around to hear him. But the Pharisees and the teachers of the law muttered, "This man welcomes sinners and eats with them."
   Luke 15:3–7. *(the parable of the lost sheep)*
   Luke 15:8–10. *(the parable of the lost coin)*
   Luke 15:11–31. *(the parable of the prodigal son)*

5. **The Samaritan woman at Jacob's well.**
   John 4:1–26.

6. **The murderer on the cross.**
   Luke 23:39–43.
   Luke 23:43. Jesus answered him, "I tell you the truth, today you will be with me in paradise."

165

7. **Saul, the persecutor of the church, who became Paul, the great missionary.**

Acts 9:1–19. *(Paul's conversion)*

1 Tim. 1:13–16. Even though I was once a blasphemer and a persecutor and a violent man, I was shown mercy because I acted in ignorance and unbelief. The grace of our Lord was poured out on me abundantly, along with the faith and love that are in Christ Jesus. Here is a trustworthy saying that deserves full acceptance: Christ Jesus came into the world to save sinners—of whom I am the worst. But for that very reason I was shown mercy so that in me, the worst of sinners, Christ Jesus might display his unlimited patience as an example for those who would believe on him and receive eternal life.

8. **The Philippian jailer.**

Acts 16:25–26.

Acts 16:30–31. He then brought them out and asked, "Sirs, what must I do to be saved?" They replied, "Believe in the Lord Jesus, and you will be saved—you and your household."

The Lord calls sinners like you and me.

1. **God calls those who are spiritually hungry and thirsty.**

Isa. 55:1–3. "Come, all you who are thirsty, come to the waters; and you who have no money, come, buy and eat! Come, buy wine and milk without money and without cost. Why spend money on what is not bread, and your labor on what does not satisfy? Listen, listen to me, and eat what is good, and your soul will delight in the richest of fare. Give ear and come to me; hear me, that your soul may live. I will make an everlasting covenant with you, my faithful love promised to David."

2. **Jesus is the bread of life and the living water, and he calls sinners to come to him.**

John 6:35. Then Jesus declared, "I am the bread of life. He who comes to me will never go hungry, and he who believes in me will never be thirsty."

John 7:37–38. On the last and greatest day of the Feast, Jesus stood and said in a loud voice, "If a man is thirsty, let him come to me and drink. Whoever believes in me, as the Scripture has said, streams of living water will flow from within him."

Rev. 22:17. The Spirit and the bride say, "Come!" And let him who hears say, "Come!" Whoever is thirsty, let him come; and whoever wishes, let him take the free gift of the water of life.

3. Jesus calls those who are weary and burdened.

Matt. 11:28–30. Come to me, all you who are weary and burdened, and I will give you rest. Take my yoke upon you and learn from me, for I am gentle and humble in heart, and you will find rest for your souls. For my yoke is easy and my burden is light.

4. He calls us to enter through the narrow gate.

Matt. 7:13–14. Enter through the narrow gate. For wide is the gate and broad is the road that leads to destruction, and many enter through it. But small is the gate and narrow the road that leads to life, and only a few find it.

5. He calls us to repent and believe the gospel.

Mark 1:14–15. After John was put in prison, Jesus went into Galilee, proclaiming the good news of God. "The time has come," he said. "The kingdom of God is near. Repent and believe the good news!"

6. Seek the Lord while he may be found.

Isa. 55:6–7. Seek the LORD while he may be found; call on him while he is near. Let the wicked forsake his way and the evil man his thoughts. Let him turn to the LORD, and he will have mercy on him, and to our God, for he will freely pardon.

7. Today, if you hear his voice, don't harden your heart.

Heb. 3:7–19.

Heb. 3:7–9. So, as the Holy Spirit says: "Today, if you hear his voice, do not harden your hearts as you did in the rebellion, during the time of testing in the desert, where your fathers tested and tried me and for forty years saw what I did."

8. The Lord will never turn a sinner away.

John 6:37. All that the Father gives me will come to me, and whoever comes to me I will never drive away.

Rom. 10:13. Everyone who calls on the name of the Lord will be saved.

We are saved to joyfully obey and serve the Lord.

1. **Offer yourself as a living sacrifice unto God.**

   Rom. 12:1–2. I urge you, brothers, in view of God's mercy, to offer your bodies as living sacrifices, holy and pleasing to God—which is your spiritual worship. Do not conform any longer to the pattern of this world, but be transformed by the renewing of your mind. Then you will be able to test and approve what God's will is—his good, pleasing and perfect will.

2. **We are saved to bear much fruit, through Jesus Christ, the vine.**
   John 15:1–8.

   John 15:8. This is my Father's glory, that you bear much fruit, showing yourselves to be my disciples.

3. **We are saved to be dead to sin, alive to God, and slaves to righteousness.**

   Rom. 6:1–23.

4. **We are called to live a new life through the power of the Holy Spirit.**

   Rom. 8:1–14.
   Eph. 5:1–21.

5. **The Holy Spirit helps us to bear fruit.**
   Gal. 5:13–26.

6. **Christ died for us so that we should no longer live for ourselves but for him.**

   2 Cor. 5:15. And he died for all, that those who live should no longer live for themselves but for him who died for them and was raised again.

   For more Scriptures on living the life of gratitude for our salvation see Loving God, p. 101; Loving and Serving Others, p. 96; Obedience, p. 111; and Progressive Sanctification, p. 141.

Self-Centeredness

See also Loving and Serving Others, p. 96, as the opposite of self-centeredness.

1. **Love is not self-seeking.**

   1 Cor. 13:5. [Love] is not rude, it is not self-seeking, it is not easily angered.

2. **Selfish ambition brings its bitter fruit.**

   James 3:14–16. If you harbor bitter envy and selfish ambition in your hearts, do not boast about it or deny the truth. Such "wisdom" does not come down from heaven but is earthly, unspiritual, of the devil. For where you have envy and selfish ambition, there you find disorder and every evil practice.

3. **Jesus condemned James and John for their self-seeking attitude, and he calls us all to humble service.**

   Matt. 20:20–28.

   Matt. 20:26–28. Whoever wants to become great among you must be your servant, and whoever wants to be first must be your slave—just as the Son of Man did not come to be served, but to serve, and to give his life as a ransom for many.

4. **Jesus calls us to self-denial.**

   Luke 9:23–25. Then he said to them all: "If anyone would come after me, he must deny himself and take up his cross daily and follow me. For whoever wants to save his life will lose it, but whoever loses his life for me will save it. What good is it for a man to gain the whole world, and yet lose or forfeit his very self?"

5. **Don't be self-centered, but think of others.**

   1 Cor. 10:24. Nobody should seek his own good, but the good of others.

6. **Follow Jesus' example by thinking of how to please others.**

   Rom. 15:2–3. Each of us should please his neighbor for his good, to build him up. For even Christ did not please himself.

7. **Do not just think of yourself. Be like Jesus, think also of others. Be self-giving.**

   Phil. 2:3–8.

   Phil. 2:3–5. Do nothing out of selfish ambition or vain conceit, but in humility consider others better than yourselves. Each of you should look not only to your own interests, but also to the interests of others. Your attitude should be the same as that of Christ Jesus.

Self-Control, Self-Discipline

1. **Lack of self-control brings misery.**

   Prov. 25:28. Like a city whose walls are broken down is a man who lacks self-control.

2. **One who gives full vent to his anger acts like a fool; one who keeps himself under control is wise.**

   Prov. 29:11. A fool gives full vent to his anger, but a wise man keeps himself under control.

3. **Every Christian can be self-controlled; it's a fruit of the Spirit.**

   Gal. 5:22–23. The fruit of the Spirit is . . . gentleness and self-control.

4. **Self-discipline is a gift of God.**

   2 Tim. 1:7. God did not give us a spirit of timidity, but a spirit of power, of love and of self-discipline.

5. **We are commanded to be self-controlled.**

   1 Peter 1:13. Prepare your minds for action; be self-controlled.

6. **One can and must develop self-control—put a lot of effort into it.**

   2 Peter 1:5–6. Make every effort to add to your faith goodness; and to goodness, knowledge; and to knowledge, self-control; and to self-control, perseverance; and to perseverance, godliness.

7. **Both old and young alike must learn self-control.**

   Titus 2:2–6. Teach the older men to be temperate, worthy of respect, self-controlled, and sound in faith, in love and in endurance. Likewise, teach the older women to be reverent in the way they live, not to be slanderers or addicted to much wine, but to teach what is good. Then they can train the younger women to love their husbands and children, to be self-controlled and pure, to be busy at home, to be kind, and to be subject to their husbands, so that no one will malign the word of God. Similarly, encourage the young men to be self-controlled.

8. **There is a time for everything. To be self-controlled is to do everything in its time.**

    Eccles. 3:1–8.

9. **We can control our thinking.**

    2 Cor. 10:5. We demolish arguments and every pretension that sets itself up against the knowledge of God, and we take captive every thought to make it obedient to Christ.

10. **Exercising self-control is walking in the light.**

    1 Thess. 5:4–8. You, brothers, are not in darkness so that this day should surprise you like a thief. You are all sons of the light and sons of the day. We do not belong to the night or to the darkness. So then, let us not be like others, who are asleep, but let us be alert and self-controlled. For those who sleep, sleep at night, and those who get drunk, get drunk at night. But since we belong to the day, let us be self-controlled, putting on faith and love as a breastplate, and the hope of salvation as a helmet.

11. **Be self-controlled in your talking; control your tongue.**

    Prov. 20:19. A gossip betrays a confidence; so avoid a man who talks too much.

    See also Communication, p. 41, for more on exercising self-control in talking.

12. **Exercise self-control and say no to all ungodliness.**

    Titus 2:11–12. The grace of God that brings salvation has appeared to all men. It teaches us to say no to ungodliness and wordly passions, and to live self-controlled, upright and godly lives in this present age.

13. **Be motivated by Christ's redeeming love.**

    Titus 2:13–14. . . . while we wait for the blessed hope—the glorious appearing of our great God and Savior, Jesus Christ, who gave himself for us to redeem us from all wickedness and to purify for himself a people that are his very own, eager to do what is good.

14. Be neither wishy-washy, nor easily moved by others.

1 Cor. 15:58. My dear brothers, stand firm. Let nothing move you. Always give yourselves fully to the work of the Lord, because you know that your labor in the Lord is not in vain.

Self-Pity, Brooding

1. **Elijah yielded to self-pity for a time and fled to Horeb.**

   1 Kings 19.

   1 Kings 19:4–5. He came to a broom tree, sat down under it and prayed that he might die. "I have had enough, LORD," he said. "Take my life; I am no better than my ancestors." Then he lay down under the tree and fell asleep.

2. **God confronted Elijah.**

   1 Kings 19:9. The word of the LORD came to him: "What are you doing here, Elijah?"

3. **Listen to Elijah's self-pity.**

   1 Kings 19:10. He replied, "I have been very zealous for the LORD God Almighty. The Israelites have rejected your covenant, broken down your altars, and put your prophets to death with the sword. I am the only one left, and now they are trying to kill me too."

4. **God dealt with Elijah's problem.**

   1 Kings 19:11–18.

5. **Asaph, the psalmist, also fell into the sin of self-pity for a time.**

   Ps. 73.

6. **Listen to Asaph's self-pity.**

   Ps. 73:13–14. Surely in vain have I kept my heart pure; in vain have I washed my hands in innocence. All day long I have been plagued; I have been punished every morning.

7. **Asaph recovered from his self-pity.**

   Ps. 73:15–28.

8. **The Lord directs us to a cure for self-pity.**

    Ps. 37.

9. **Turn from self-pity.**

    Prov. 15:13. A happy heart makes the face cheerful, but heartache crushes the spirit.

10. **Jonah became angry and was filled with self-pity, for which God rebuked him.**

    Jonah 4:1–4.

    Jonah 4:3–4. "Now, O LORD, take away my life, for it is better for me to die than to live." But the LORD replied, "Have you any right to be angry?"

Sex Life

See also Song of Songs.

1. **Sex is God-given.**

   Heb. 13:4. Marriage should be honored by all, and the marriage bed kept pure, for God will judge the adulterer and all the sexually immoral.

2. **Fulfill your duty to your spouse.**

   1 Cor. 7:3. The husband should fulfill his marital duty to his wife, and likewise the wife to her husband.

3. **Your body also belongs to your spouse.**

   1 Cor. 7:4. The wife's body does not belong to her alone but also to her husband. In the same way, the husband's body does not belong to him alone but also to his wife.

4. **Refrain only by mutual consent; for refraining can lead to temptation.**

   1 Cor. 7:5. Do not deprive each other except by mutual consent and for a time, so that you may devote yourselves to prayer. Then come together again so that Satan will not tempt you because of your lack of self-control.

5. **Find satisfaction in your spouse.**

   Prov. 5:18–20. May your fountain be blessed, and may you rejoice in the wife of your youth. A loving doe, a graceful deer—may her breasts satisfy you always, may you ever be captivated by her love. Why be captivated, my son, by an adulteress? Why embrace the bosom of another man's wife?

Sexual Immorality

See also Adultery, p. 9; and Homosexuality, p. 88.

1. **Looking on a woman lustfully is adulterous.**

   Matt. 5:27–28. You have heard that it was said, "Do not commit adultery." But I tell you that anyone who looks at a woman lustfully has already committed adultery with her in his heart.

2. **Spiritual surgery may be needed to avoid immorality.**

   Matt. 5:29–30. If your right eye causes you to sin, gouge it out and throw it away. It is better for you to lose one part of your body than for your whole body to be thrown into hell.

3. **Put to death sexual immorality.**

   Col. 3:5–7. Put to death, therefore, whatever belongs to your earthly nature: sexual immorality, impurity, lust, evil desires and greed, which is idolatry. Because of these, the wrath of God is coming. You used to walk in these ways, in the life you once lived.

4. **You can overcome sins of sexual immorality.**

   Prov. 4:23. Above all else, guard your heart, for it is the wellspring of life.

   Prov. 4:24–27. Put away perversity from your mouth; keep corrupt talk far from your lips. Let your eyes look straight ahead, fix your gaze directly before you. Make level paths for your feet and take only ways that are firm. Do not swerve to the right or left; keep your foot from evil.

5. **Sexual sins come from the heart.**

   Matt. 15:19–20. Out of the heart come evil thoughts, murder, adultery, sexual immorality.

6. **Sexual immorality, including premarital sex (fornication), is described in detail as sin against God and your body, the temple of the Holy Spirit.**

    1 Cor. 6:12–20.

7. **The sexually immoral will not inherit the kingdom of God.**

    1 Cor. 6:9–10. Do you not know that the wicked will not inherit the kingdom of God? Do not be deceived: Neither the sexually immoral nor idolaters nor adulterers nor male prostitutes nor homosexual offenders nor thieves nor the greedy nor drunkards nor slanderers nor swindlers will inherit the kingdom of God.

8. **God can cleanse you from the sin of sexual immorality.**

    1 Cor. 6:11. And that is what some of you were. But you were washed, you were sanctified, you were justified in the name of the Lord Jesus Christ and by the Spirit of our God.

9. **You can overcome sexual immorality through the Holy Spirit.**

    Gal. 5:16–18. So I say, live by the Spirit, and you will not gratify the desires of the sinful nature. For the sinful nature desires what is contrary to the Spirit, and the Spirit what is contrary to the sinful nature. They are in conflict with each other, so that you do not do what you want. But if you are led by the Spirit, you are not under law.

10. **All immorality is forbidden. Walk as children of light. Be very careful how you live.**

    Eph. 5:3–17.

11. **Jesus can set you free.**

    John 8:31–36.

12. **Purify yourself out of reverence for God.**

    2 Cor. 7:1. Since we have these promises, dear friends, let us purify ourselves from everything that contaminates body and spirit, perfecting holiness out of reverence for God.

13. **Christians must no longer use parts of the body for sin; one can and must change.**

    Rom. 6:15–23.

14. **The destruction of Sodom and Gomorrah is a warning for all sexually immoral people.**

    2 Peter 2:4–10.

    Jude 6–7. The angels who did not keep their positions of authority but abandoned their own home—these he kept in darkness, bound with everlasting chains for judgment on the great Day. In a similar way, Sodom and Gomorrah and the surrounding towns gave themselves up to sexual immorality and perversion. They serve as an example of those who suffer the punishment of eternal fire.

15. **God wants all of us to avoid sexual immorality, including premarital sex, and to learn to control our own bodies.**

    1 Thess. 4:3–6. It is God's will that you should be holy; that you should avoid sexual immorality; that each of you should learn to control his own body in a way that is holy and honorable, not in passionate lust like the heathen, who do not know God; and that in this matter no one should wrong his brother or take advantage of him. The Lord will punish men for all such sins, as we have already told you and warned you.

Temptation

See also Overcoming Sin, p. 117; and Progressive Sanctification, p. 141.

1. **Satan subtly tempted Eve.**

    Gen. 3:1–4. Now the serpent was more crafty than any of the wild animals the LORD God had made. He said to the woman, "Did God really say, 'You must not eat from any tree in the garden'?" The woman said to the serpent, "We may eat fruit from the trees in the garden, but God did say, 'You must not eat fruit from the tree that is in the middle of the garden, and you must not touch it, or you will die.'" "You will not surely die," the serpent said to the woman.

2. **The devil still prowls around like a lion, seeking whom he may devour.**

    1 Peter 5:8–9. Be self-controlled and alert. Your enemy the devil prowls around like a roaring lion looking for someone to devour. Resist him, standing firm in the faith, because you know that your brothers throughout the world are undergoing the same kind of sufferings.

3. **Satan at times comes as an angel of light.**

    2 Cor. 11:14–15. Satan himself masquerades as an angel of light. It is not surprising, then, if his servants masquerade as servants of righteousness. Their end will be what their actions deserve.

4. **At times, Satan uses others to entice us.**

    Prov. 1:10. My son, if sinners entice you, do not give in to them.

5. **God tempts no one. Each one is tempted when, by his own desire, he is dragged away and enticed.**

    James 1:13–15. When tempted, no one should say, "God is tempting me." For God cannot be tempted by evil, nor does he tempt anyone; but each one is tempted when, by his own evil desire, he is dragged away and enticed. Then, after desire has conceived, it gives birth to sin; and sin, when it is full-grown, gives birth to death.

6. **Resist the devil.**

James 4:7. Submit yourselves, then, to God. Resist the devil, and he will flee from you.

7. **Jesus was tempted by the devil.**

Matt. 4:1–11.

8. **Jesus won by using the sword of the Spirit, God's Word, each time.**

Matt. 4:4, 7, 10. *(Each time Jesus said, "It is written . . .")*

9. **Jesus tells us to watch and pray, lest we should yield to temptation.**

Matt. 6:13. And lead us not into temptation, but deliver us from the evil one.

Matt. 26:41. Watch and pray so that you will not fall into temptation. The spirit is willing, but the body is weak.

10. **Every Christian should take heed, lest he or she should fall.**

1 Cor. 10:12. So, if you think you are standing firm, be careful that you don't fall!

11. **Put on the whole armor of God to fight against the devil's schemes.**

Eph. 6:10–18.

Eph. 6:10–12. Finally, be strong in the Lord and in his mighty power. Put on the full armor of God so that you can take your stand against the devil's schemes. For our struggle is not against flesh and blood, but against the rulers, against the authorities, against the powers of this dark world and against the spiritual forces of evil in the heavenly realms.

12. **When he was tempted by Potiphar's wife to commit adultery, Joseph refused to sin against God.**

Gen. 39:6–20.

Gen. 39:9–10. "How then could I do such a wicked thing and sin against God?" And though she spoke to Joseph day after day, he refused to go to bed with her or even be with her.

Training Children

See also Youth, p. 204.

1. **God requires parents to rear their children in a God-centered way. The primary objective must be that your children know, believe in, love, reverence, and serve the Lord.**

    Deut. 6:6–7. These commandments that I give you today are to be upon your hearts. Impress them on your children. Talk about them when you sit at home and when you walk along the road, when you lie down and when you get up.

    John 17:3. Now this is eternal life: that they may know you, the only true God, and Jesus Christ, whom you have sent.

    Eph. 6:4. Fathers, do not exasperate your children; instead, bring them up in the training and instruction of the Lord.

2. **The father is primarily responsible for child training.**

    Eph. 6:4.

3. **Like the psalmist David, all children are conceived and born in sin. Parents must seek to lead them to a saving knowledge of Jesus Christ.**

    Ps. 51:5. Surely I was sinful at birth, sinful from the time my mother conceived me.

4. **Parents must shepherd the child's heart, not only discipline, not merely attempt to correct outward behavior. When anyone sins it arises out of the heart.**

    Prov. 4:23. Above all else, guard your heart, for it is the well-spring of life.

Mark 7:21–23. For from within, out of men's hearts, come evil thoughts, sexual immorality, theft, murder, adultery, greed, malice, deceit, lewdness, envy, slander, arrogance and folly. All these evils come from inside and make a man "unclean."

5. **Much of a child's sinful behavior arises out of a self-centered, selfish attitude.**

See also Loving and Serving Others, p. 96; and Self-Centeredness, p. 169.

6. **Parents must give biblical instruction to their children, not just lay down rules and expectations.**
    Deut. 6:6–7; Eph. 6:4. *(See #1 on p. 182.)*
    Prov. 1:8–9. Listen, my son, to your father's instruction and do not forsake your mother's teaching. They will be a garland to grace your head and a chain to adorn your neck.

7. **The Holy Spirit works through the word of God to develop spiritual growth, biblical change in the lives of children and adults alike. Jesus prayed for this work of grace in his high priestly prayer.**
    John 17:17. Sanctify them from the truth; your word is truth.

8. **Your parental calling is similar to that which God gave to Abraham, the father of believers.**
    Gen. 18:19. For I have chosen him, so that he will direct his children and his household after him to keep the way of the LORD by doing what is right and just, so that the LORD will bring about for Abraham what he has promised him.

9. **Parents must set a godly example for their children to learn by and to follow.**
    Deut. 6:4–6. Hear, O Israel: The LORD our God, the LORD is one. Love the LORD your God with all your heart and with all your soul and with all your strength. These commandments that I give you today are to be upon your hearts.

10. **The father must manage his family well and see that his children obey him with proper respect.**
    1 Tim. 3:4. He must manage his own family well and see that his children obey him with proper respect.

11. **Do not exasperate your children by unjust requirements or undue discipline.**

    Eph. 6:4. *(See #1 on p. 182.)*

    Col. 3:21. Fathers, do not embitter your children, or they will become discouraged.

12. **Love requires faithful discipline.**

    Prov. 13:24. He who spares the rod hates his son, but he who loves him is careful to discipline him.

    Prov. 22:15. Folly is bound up in the heart of a child, but the rod of discipline will drive it far from him.

    Prov. 23:13–14. Do not withhold discipline from a child; if you punish him with the rod, he will not die. Punish him with the rod and save his soul from death.

    Prov. 29:15. The rod of correction imparts wisdom, but a child left to itself disgraces his mother.

    Prov. 29:17. Discipline your son, and he will give you peace; he will bring delight to your soul.

13. **Follow God's pattern, for he lovingly disciplines his children for their good.**

    Heb. 12:5–11.

14. **He is motivated by love for his children.**

    Heb. 12:6. [T]he Lord disciplines those he loves, and he punishes everyone he accepts as a son.

15. **God intends for discipline to be painful. He always does it for our good, that it may bear rich fruit in our lives.**

    Heb. 12:11. No discipline seems pleasant at the time, but painful. Later on, however, it produces a harvest of righteousness and peace for those who have been trained by it.

16. **The Lord condemned Eli for being an indulgent parent.**

    1 Sam. 3:1–18.

    1 Sam. 3:13. I told him that I would judge his family forever because of the sin he knew about; his sons made themselves contemptible, and he failed to restrain them.

17. **Train a child in the way he should go.**

    Prov. 22:6. Train a child in the way he should go, and when he is old he will not turn from it.

18. Unless the Lord builds the house . . .

Ps. 127:1–2. Unless the LORD builds the house, its builders labor in vain. Unless the LORD watches over the city, the watchmen stand guard in vain. In vain you rise early and stay up late, toiling for food to eat—for he grants sleep to those he loves.

19. Children are a heritage from the Lord.

Ps. 127:3. Sons are a heritage from the LORD, children a reward from him.

Trust, Faith in God

See also Comfort, p. 37; Fear, p. 70; and Providence of God, p. 146.

1. **Trust in the Lord.**

    Prov. 3:5–6. Trust in the LORD with all your heart, and lean not on your own understanding; in all your ways acknowledge him, and he will make your paths straight.

2. **Nothing is too hard for God.**

    Jer. 32:17, 26–27. "Ah, Sovereign LORD, you have made the heavens and the earth by your great power and outstretched arm. Nothing is too hard for you. . . ." Then the word of the LORD came to Jeremiah: "I am the LORD, the God of all mankind. Is anything too hard for me?"

3. **See the glory and power of God.**

    1 Chron. 29:10–13.

    1 Chron. 29:11–12. Yours, O LORD, is the greatness and the power and the glory and the majesty and the splendor, for everything in heaven and earth is yours. Yours, O LORD, is the kingdom; you are exalted as head over all. Wealth and honor come from you; you are the ruler of all things. In your hands are strength and power to exalt and give strength to all.

4. **The Lord is your shepherd.**

    Ps. 23.

5. **The Lord is the believer's light and his salvation.**

    Ps. 27. *(See the entire psalm; notice especially vv. 1, 2, 5, 7, 8, 13, 14.)*
    Ps. 27:8. My heart says of you, "Seek his face!" Your face, LORD, I will seek.

Ps. 27:13–14. I am still confident of this: I will see the goodness of the LORD in the land of the living. Wait for the LORD; be strong and take heart and wait for the LORD.

6. **The Lord is the believer's refuge and strength.**

   Ps. 91:1–2. He who dwells in the shelter of the Most High will rest in the shadow of the Almighty. I will say of the LORD, "He is my refuge and my fortress, my God, in whom I trust."

7. **Lift your eyes to the hills.**

   Ps. 121. *(See the entire psalm, which teaches so beautifully that the Lord is our helper, the one who watches over us and keeps us.)*

8. **Jesus calmed the storm and rebuked the disciples for their little faith.**

   Matt. 8:23–27.

9. **Jesus rebuked Peter for his little faith.**

   Matt. 14:22–31. *(Jesus walked on water; Peter tried and failed.)*
   Matt. 14:31. Immediately Jesus reached out his hand and caught him. "You of little faith," he said, "why did you doubt?"

10. **God is faithful; his mercies are new every morning.**

    Lam. 3:22–24. Because of the LORD's great love we are not consumed, for his compassions never fail. They are new every morning; great is your faithfulness. I say to myself, "The LORD is my portion; therefore I will wait for him."

11. **God is always faithful.**

    Lam. 3:32. Though he brings grief, he will show compassion, so great is his unfailing love.

12. **Trust and delight in the Lord; wait patiently for him.**

    Ps. 37:1–7.
    Ps. 37:3. Trust in the LORD and do good; dwell in the land and enjoy safe pasture.
    Ps. 37:4. Delight yourself in the LORD and he will give you the desires of your heart.
    Ps. 37:5–6. Commit your way to the LORD; trust in him and he will do this: He will make your righteousness shine like the dawn.
    Ps. 37:7. Be still before the LORD and wait patiently for him.

13. **Why are you downcast? Hope in God!**

    Ps. 42.

    Ps. 42:5. Why are you downcast, O my soul? Why so disturbed within me? Put your hope in God, for I will yet praise him, my Savior and my God.

14. **God is our refuge and strength.**

    Ps. 46.

15. **God knows us intimately; he is always leading us.**

    Ps. 139:1–11.

    Ps. 139:1–3. O LORD, you have searched me and you know me. You know when I sit and when I rise; you perceive my thoughts from afar. You discern my going out and my lying down; you are familiar with all my ways.

    Ps. 139:9–10. If I rise on the wings of the dawn, if I settle on the far side of the sea, even there your hand will guide me, your right hand will hold me fast.

16. **God holds and guides us.**

    Ps. 73:23–24. I am always with you; you hold me by my right hand. You guide me with your counsel, and afterward you will take me into glory.

17. **Be near to God, your refuge.**

    Ps. 73:28. As for me, it is good to be near God. I have made the Sovereign LORD my refuge; I will tell of all your deeds.

18. **God gives comfort to his people, and encourages them to put their trust in him.**

    Isa. 40.

    Isa. 40:11. He tends his flock like a shepherd: He gathers the lambs in his arms and carries them close to his heart; he gently leads those that have young.

    Isa. 40:28–31. Do you not know? Have you not heard? The LORD is the everlasting God, the Creator of the ends of the earth. He will not grow tired or weary, and his understanding no one can fathom. He gives strength to the weary and increases the power of the weak. Even youths grow tired and weary and young men stumble and fall; but those who hope in the LORD will renew their strength.

They will soar on wings like eagles; they will run and not grow weary, they will walk and not be faint.

19. **Do not fear; you are the Lord's child.**

    Isa. 43:1–3. Fear not, for I have redeemed you; I have called you by name; you are mine. When you pass through the waters I will be with you; and when you pass through the rivers, they will not sweep over you; when you walk through the fire, you will not be burned; the flames will not set you ablaze. For I am the LORD, your God, the Holy One of Israel, your Savior.

20. **Do not fear; the Lord is with you.**

    Isa. 41:10. Do not fear, for I am with you; do not be dismayed, for I am your God. I will strengthen you and help you; I will uphold you with my righteous right hand.

21. **Call upon the Lord in the day of trouble.**

    Ps. 50:15. Call upon me in the day of trouble; I will deliver you, and you will honor me.

22. **Take refuge in the Lord.**

    Ps. 57:1. Have mercy on me, O God, have mercy on me, for in you my soul takes refuge. I will take refuge in the shadow of your wings until the disaster has passed.

23. **Trust your heavenly Father to take care of you. Think of how God cares even for the birds and the flowers. You are of much more value than they.**

    Matt. 6:25–34.

24. **God's servant Joshua is given a difficult task. The Lord counsels him to be strong and courageous.**

    Josh. 1:1–9.

    Josh. 1:9. Have I not commanded you? Be strong and courageous. Do not be terrified; do not be discouraged, for the LORD your God will be with you wherever you go.

25. **Trust in the Lord brings peace to the heart. Trust in his unfailing love.**

    Isa. 26:3–4. You will keep in perfect peace him whose mind is steadfast, because he trusts in you. Trust in the LORD forever, for the LORD, the LORD, is the Rock eternal.

Ps. 9:9. The LORD is a refuge for the oppressed, a stronghold in times of trouble.

Ps. 28:7–8. The LORD is my strength and my shield; my heart trusts in him, and I am helped. My heart leaps for joy and I will give thanks to him in song. The LORD is the strength of his people, a fortress of salvation for his anointed one.

Ps. 33:18–22. The eyes of the LORD are on those who fear him, on those whose hope is in his unfailing love, to deliver them from death and keep them alive in famine. We wait in hope for the LORD; he is our help and our shield. In him our hearts rejoice, for we trust in his holy name. May your unfailing love rest upon us, O LORD, even as we put our hope in you.

Ps. 36:5–9. Your love, O LORD, reaches to the heavens, your faithfulness to the skies. Your righteousness is like the mighty mountains, your justice like the great deep. O LORD, you preserve both man and beast. How priceless is your unfailing love! Both high and low among men find refuge in the shadow of your wings. They feast on the abundance of your house; you give them drink from your river of delights. For with you is the fountain of life; in your light we see light.

26. God cares for those who trust in him.

Nahum 1:7. The LORD is good, a refuge in times of trouble. He cares for those who trust in him.

27. Do not trust in worldly power or wicked men.

Isa. 31:1. Woe to those who go down to Egypt for help, who rely on horses, who trust in the multitude of their chariots and in the great strength of their horsemen, but do not look to the Holy One of Israel, or seek help from the LORD.

Jer. 17:7–8. But blessed is the man who trusts in the LORD, whose confidence is in him. He will be like a tree planted by the water that sends out its roots by the stream.

28. God cannot forget us.

Isa. 49:14–16. Zion said, "The LORD has forsaken me, the LORD has forgotten me." "Can a mother forget the baby at her breast and have no compassion on the child she has borne? Though she may forget, I will not forget you! See, I have engraved you on the palms of my hands; your walls are ever before me."

29. **Find rest in God alone. Trust in him at all times, under any and all circumstances.**

    Ps. 62:5–8. Find rest, O my soul, in God alone; my hope comes from him. He alone is my rock and my salvation; he is my fortress, I will not be shaken. My salvation and my honor depend on God; he is my mighty rock, my refuge.

30. **The Lord takes delight in those who fear him and trust in his unfailing love.**

    Ps. 147:11. The LORD delights in those who fear him, who put their hope in his unfailing love.

31. **Keep trusting in God's unfailing love even when a desired blessing seems to be so slow, so long in coming.**

    Ps. 13.

    Ps. 13:1. How long, O LORD? Will you forget me forever? How long will you hide your face from me?

    Ps. 13:5–6. But I trust in your unfailing love; my heart rejoices in your salvation. I will sing to the LORD, for he has been good to me.

32. **God's people were rebuked and judged for not trusting the Lord to bring them safely into the promised land after he had led them so marvelously on their pilgrim journey.**

    Deut. 1:26–36.

    Deut. 1:32–33. In spite of this, you did not trust in the LORD your God, who went ahead of you on your journey, in fire by night and in a cloud by day, to search out places for you to camp and to show you the way you should go.

Warnings, Calls to Repentance and Obedience

See also Repentance, p. 153; Obedience, p. 111.

Note: Many warnings are coupled with promises from God to those who trust in him and serve him faithfully.

1. **The way of sin leads to death; the way of obedience to life.**

   Matt. 7:13–14. Enter through the narrow gate. For wide is the gate and broad is the road that leads to destruction, and many enter through it. But small is the gate and narrow the road that leads to life, and only a few find it.

2. **Only those who hear and obey God's Word will have life.**

   Matt. 7:21–23. Not everyone who says to me, "Lord, Lord," will enter the kingdom of heaven, but only he who does the will of my Father who is in heaven. Many will say to me on that day, "Lord, Lord, did we not prophesy in your name, and in your name drive out demons and perform many miracles?" Then I will tell them plainly, "I never knew you. Away from me, you evildoers!"

3. **Jesus gave us the parable of the wise and the foolish builders.**

   Matt. 7:24–27. Everyone who hears these words of mine and puts them into practice is like a wise man who built his house on the rock. The rain came down, the streams rose, and the winds blew and beat against that house; yet it did not fall, because it had its foundation on the rock. But everyone who hears these words of mine and does not put them into practice is like a foolish man who built his house on sand. The rain came down, the streams rose, and the winds blew and beat against that house, and it fell with a great crash.

4. **You will reap what you sow.**

   Prov. 22:5. In the paths of the wicked lie thorns and snares, but he who guards his soul stays far from them.

   Prov. 11:19–21. The truly righteous man attains life, but he who pursues evil goes to his death. The LORD detests men of perverse heart but he delights in those whose ways are blameless. Be sure of this: The wicked will not go unpunished, but those who are righteous will go free.

   Gal. 6:7–8. Do not be deceived: God cannot be mocked. A man reaps what he sows. The one who sows to please his sinful nature, from that nature will reap destruction; the one who sows to please the Spirit, from the Spirit will reap eternal life.

5. **No one can serve two masters—God will not accept a double life.**

   Matt. 6:24. No one can serve two masters. Either he will hate the one and love the other, or he will be devoted to the one and despise the other. You cannot serve both God and Money.

6. **God rejects the worship of one who is living in sin.**

   Prov. 15:8. The LORD detests the sacrifice of the wicked, but the prayer of the upright pleases him.

   Prov. 15:29. The LORD is far from the wicked but he hears the prayer of the righteous.

   Prov. 21:27. The sacrifice of the wicked is detestable—how much more so when brought with evil intent!

   Prov. 28:9. If anyone turns a deaf ear to the law, even his prayers are detestable.

7. **If you keep ignoring God's call to repentance, he will laugh at your calamity.**

   Prov. 1:24–33.

8. **The Lord curses the wicked, but he blesses the righteous.**

   Prov. 3:33. The LORD's curse is on the house of the wicked, but he blesses the home of the righteous.

9. **The wages of sin is death.**

   Rom. 6:23. The wages of sin is death, but the gift of God is eternal life in Christ Jesus our Lord.

10. We are warned not to drift away from the Lord.

Heb. 2:1–3. We must pay more careful attention, therefore, to what we have heard, so that we do not drift away. For if the message spoken by angels was binding, and every violation and disobedience received its just punishment, how shall we escape if we ignore such a great salvation? This salvation, which was first announced by the Lord, was confirmed to us by those who heard him.

11. We are warned not to fall away.

Heb. 6:4–6. It is impossible for those who have once been enlightened, who have tasted the heavenly gift, who have shared in the Holy Spirit, who have tasted the goodness of the word of God and the powers of the coming age, if they fall away, to be brought back to repentance, because to their loss they are crucifying the Son of God all over again and subjecting him to public disgrace.

12. Those who have known the way but go on sinning are warned of the consequences.

Heb. 10:26–31.

Heb. 10:26–27. If we deliberately keep on sinning after we have received the knowledge of the truth, no sacrifice for sins is left, but only a fearful expectation of judgment and of raging fire that will consume the enemies of God.

Heb. 10:31. It is a dreadful thing to fall into the hands of the living God.

13. Don't harden your heart; listen to his voice today.

Heb. 3:7–15.

Heb. 3:7–8. As the Holy Spirit says: "Today, if you hear his voice, do not harden your hearts as you did in the rebellion."

14. On the judgment day Jesus will separate the sheep from the goats.

Matt. 25:31–46.

Matt. 25:34. Then the King will say to those on his right, "Come, you who are blessed by my Father; take your inheritance, the kingdom prepared for you since the creation of the world."

Matt. 25:41. Then he will say to those on his left, "Depart from me, you who are cursed, into the eternal fire prepared for the devil and his angels."

Matt. 25:46. Then they will go away to eternal punishment, but the righteous to eternal life.

15. What if you gain the whole world and lose your soul?

Matt. 16:26–27. What good will it be for a man if he gains the whole world, yet forfeits his soul? Or what can a man give in exchange for his soul? For the Son of Man is going to come in his Father's glory with his angels, and then he will reward each person according to what he has done.

16. We will all appear before the judgment seat of Christ.

2 Cor. 5:10. We must all appear before the judgment seat of Christ, that each one may receive what is due him for the things done while in the body, whether good or bad.

17. Always be prepared for Jesus' return, for the day and hour are not known.

Mark 13:32–37. No one knows about that day or hour, not even the angels in heaven, nor the Son, but only the Father. Be on guard! Be alert! You do not know when that time will come. It's like a man going away: He leaves his house in charge of his servants, each with his assigned task, and tells the one at the door to keep watch. Therefore keep watch because you do not know when the owner of the house will come back—whether in the evening, or at midnight, or when the rooster crows, or at dawn. If he comes suddenly, do not let him find you sleeping. What I say to you, I say to everyone: "Watch!"

18. Jesus gave us the parable of the ten virgins.

Matt. 25:1–13.

19. Only those who believe in Jesus will be saved.

John 3:16–18. God so loved the world that he gave his one and only Son, that whoever believes in him shall not perish but have eternal life. For God did not send his Son into the world to condemn the world, but to save the world through him. Whoever believes in him is not condemned, but whoever does not believe stands condemned already because he has not believed in the name of God's one and only Son.

20. **Blessed is the man who does not walk in the way of the wicked. The wicked will not stand in the day of judgment.**

    Ps. 1.

21. **God's judgment by the flood and the destruction of Sodom and Gomorrah are set forth as a warning to sinners today.**

    2 Peter 2:4–10.
    Jude 6–7, 14–15.

22. **The history of others is recorded as a warning for us.**

    1 Cor. 10:11–12. These things happened to them [the Israelites] as examples and were written down as warnings for us, on whom the fulfillment of the ages has come. So, if you think you are standing firm, be careful that you don't fall!

23. **God punishes the guilty.**

    Nahum 1:1–6.

    Nahum 1:2–3. The LORD is a jealous and avenging God; the LORD takes vengeance and is filled with wrath. The LORD takes vengeance on his foes and maintains his wrath against his enemies. The LORD is slow to anger and great in power; the LORD will not leave the guilty unpunished. His way is in the whirlwind and the storm, and clouds are the dust of his feet.

24. **Woe to those who call evil good and good evil.**

    Isa. 5:20–21. Woe to those who call evil good and good evil, who put darkness for light and light for darkness, who put bitter for sweet and sweet for bitter. Woe to those who are wise in their own eyes and clever in their own sight.

25. **One who has known the Way but turns away from the Lord will receive greater condemnation.**

    2 Peter 2:20–22. If they have escaped the corruption of the world by knowing our Lord and Savior Jesus Christ and are again entangled in it and overcome, they are worse off at the end than they were at the beginning. It would have been better for them not to have known the way of righteousness, than to have known it and then to turn their backs on the sacred commandment that was passed on to them. Of them the proverbs are true: "A dog returns to its vomit," and, "A sow that is washed goes back to her wallowing in the mud."

26. **Unrepented sin separates a person from God.**

Isa. 59:1–2. Surely the arm of the LORD is not too short to save, nor his ear too dull to hear. But your iniquities have separated you from your God; your sins have hidden his face from you, so that he will not hear.

27. **God detests hypocritical worship coupled with ungodly living.**
   Jer. 7:1–29.

Jer. 7:2–4. Stand at the gate of the LORD's house and there proclaim this message: "Hear the word of the LORD, all you people of Judah who come through these gates to worship the LORD. This is what the LORD Almighty, the God of Israel, says: Reform your ways and your actions, and I will let you live in this place."

Jer. 7:9–11. Will you steal and murder, commit adultery and perjury, burn incense to Baal and follow other gods you have not known, and then come and stand before me in this house, which bears my Name, and say, "We are safe"—safe to do all these detestable things? Has this house, which bears my Name, become a den of robbers to you? But I have been watching! declares the LORD.

Work, Laziness

1. **At the dawn of history God called man to work as his servant.**

    Gen. 2:15. The LORD God took the man and put him in the Garden of Eden to work it and take care of it.

2. **Be a workman approved of God.**

    2 Tim. 2:15. Do your best to present yourself to God as one approved, a workman who does not need to be ashamed and who correctly handles the word of truth.

3. **Do everything to the glory of God; perform your work in a way that glorifies him.**

    1 Cor. 10:31. Whether you eat or drink or whatever you do, do it all for the glory of God.

    Col. 3:17. Whatever you do, whether in word or deed, do it all in the name of the Lord Jesus, giving thanks to God the Father through him.

4. **An industrious housewife and mother pleases the Lord and delights her husband.**

    Prov. 31:10–31.

5. **Christians must work in order to give to others; never steal.**

    Eph. 4:28. He who has been stealing must steal no longer, but must work, doing something useful with his own hands, that he may have something to share with those in need.

6. **Be a faithful worker so that you will be a good witness to outsiders and not be dependent on others.**

    1 Thess. 4:11–12. Make it your ambition to lead a quiet life, to mind your own business and to work with your hands, just as we told you, so that your daily life may win the respect of outsiders and so that you will not be dependent on anybody.

7. **Be on guard against idleness.**

   2 Thess. 2:6–15.

   2 Thess. 3:7–10. You yourselves know how you ought to follow our example. We were not idle when we were with you, nor did we eat anyone's food without paying for it. On the contrary, we worked night and day, laboring and toiling so that we would not be a burden to any of you. We did this, not because we do not have the right to such help, but in order to make ourselves a model for you to follow. For even when we were with you, we gave you this rule: "If a man will not work, he shall not eat."

8. **Earn your own bread.**

   2 Thess. 3:12. Such people we command and urge in the Lord Jesus Christ to settle down and earn the bread they eat.

9. **The ant provides a lesson for lazy, careless people.**

   Prov. 6:6–11. Go to the ant, you sluggard; consider its ways and be wise! It has no commander, no overseer or ruler, yet it stores its provisions in summer and gathers its food at harvest. How long will you lie there, you sluggard? When will you get up from your sleep? A little sleep, a little slumber, a little folding of the hands to rest—and poverty will come on you like a bandit and scarcity like an armed man.

10. **It's a disgrace to be lazy.**

    Prov. 10:5. He who gathers crops in summer is a wise son, but he who sleeps during harvest is a disgraceful son.

11. **One who chases fantasies lacks judgment.**

    Prov. 12:11. He who works his land will have abundant food, but he who chases fantasies lacks judgment.

12. **Mere talk leads to poverty.**

    Prov. 14:23. All hard work brings a profit, but mere talk leads only to poverty.

13. **The way of the sluggard is hard.**

    Prov. 15:19. The way of the sluggard is blocked with thorns, but the path of the upright is a highway.

14. **The shiftless man goes hungry.**

    Prov. 19:15. Laziness brings on deep sleep, and the shiftless man goes hungry.

15. **Being lazy has its sad results.**

    Prov. 20:4. A sluggard does not plow in season; so at harvest time he looks but finds nothing.

16. **Do not love sleep.**

    Prov. 20:13. Do not love sleep or you will grow poor; stay awake and you will have food to spare.

17. **A shiftless sluggard will come to poverty.**

    Prov. 24:30–34. I went past the field of a sluggard, past the vineyard of the man who lacks judgment; thorns had come up everywhere, the ground was covered with weeds, and the stone wall was in ruins. I applied my heart to what I observed and learned a lesson from what I saw: A little sleep, a little slumber, a little folding of the hands to rest—and poverty will come on you like a bandit and scarcity like an armed man.

18. **The sluggard finds excuses not to work; he rationalizes his behavior.**

    Prov. 26:13–16. The sluggard says, "There is a lion in the road, a fierce lion roaming the streets!" As a door turns on its hinges, so a sluggard turns on his bed. The sluggard buries his hand in the dish; he is too lazy to bring it back to his mouth. The sluggard is wiser in his own eyes than seven men who answer discreetly.

19. **The sleep of a laborer is sweet.**

    Eccles. 5:12. The sleep of a laborer is sweet, whether he eats little or much, but the abundance of a rich man permits him no sleep.

20. **In the parable of the talents Jesus teaches us to serve him faithfully with the talents he gives to us.**

    Matt. 25:14–30.

21. **One who fails to provide for his family denies the faith.**

    1 Tim. 5:8. If anyone does not provide for his relatives, and especially for his immediate family, he has denied the faith and is worse than an unbeliever.

22. **We must learn to work so that we may provide for daily necessities and live productive lives.**

Titus 3:14. Our people must learn to devote themselves to doing what is good, in order that they may provide for daily necessities and not live unproductive lives.

Worry, Anxiety

See also Prayer, p. 137; and Trust, p. 186.

1. **Jesus instructs us not to worry about tomorrow; about food, clothing, etc.**

   Matt. 6:25–34.

   Matt. 6:25. I tell you, do not worry about your life, what you will eat or drink; or about your body, what you will wear. Is not life more important than food, and the body more important than clothes?

   Matt. 6:26, 28. Look at the birds of the air; they do not sow or reap or store away in barns, and yet your heavenly Father feeds them. . . . And why do you worry about clothes? See how the lilies of the field grow. They do not labor or spin.

2. **Take one day at a time, and don't borrow trouble.**

   Matt. 6:34. Do not worry about tomorrow, for tomorrow will worry about itself. Each day has enough trouble of its own.

3. **Don't be anxious, but pray.**

   Phil. 4:6–7. Do not be anxious about anything, but in everything, by prayer and petition, with thanksgiving, present your requests to God. And the peace of God, which transcends all understanding, will guard your hearts and your minds in Christ Jesus.

4. **Cast all your anxiety on the Lord.**

   1 Peter 5:6–7. Humble yourselves, therefore, under God's mighty hand, that he may lift you up in due time. Cast all your anxiety on him because he cares for you.

5. **You can discover the secret of tranquillity.**

   Ps. 37:3–7.
   Ps. 37:3. Trust in the LORD and do good.
   Ps. 37:4. Delight yourself in the LORD.
   Ps. 37:5. Commit your way to the LORD.
   Ps. 37:7. Be still before the LORD and wait patiently for him.

6. **Anxiety weighs a person down.**

   Prov. 12:25. An anxious heart weighs a man down, but a kind word cheers him up.

   Prov. 14:30. A heart at peace gives life to the body, but envy rots the bones.

   Prov. 17:22. A cheerful heart is good medicine, but a crushed spirit dries up the bones.

Youth

See also Forgiveness of Sins, p. 72; Friendships, p. 82; and Warnings, p. 192.

1. **Be happy, young man.**

   Eccles. 11:9–10. Be happy, young man, while you are young, and let your heart give you joy in the days of your youth. Follow the ways of your heart and whatever your eyes see, but know that for all these things God will bring you to judgment. So then, banish anxiety from your heart and cast off the troubles of your body, for youth and vigor are meaningless.

2. **Remember your Creator in the days of your youth.**

   Eccles. 12:1. Remember your Creator in the days of your youth, before the days of trouble come and the years approach when you will say, "I find no pleasure in them."

3. **Be sure to go God's way.**

   Prov. 3:1–4. My son, do not forget my teaching, but keep my commands in your heart, for they will prolong your life many years and bring you prosperity. Let love and faithfulness never leave you; bind them around your neck, write them on the tablet of your heart. Then you will win favor and a good name in the sight of God and man.

4. **Trust in the Lord; acknowledge him in all your ways.**

   Prov. 3:5–6. Trust in the LORD with all your heart and lean not on your own understanding; in all your ways acknowledge him, and he will make your paths straight.

5. **The fear of the Lord is the beginning of knowledge and wisdom.**

   Prov. 1:7. The fear of the LORD is the beginning of knowledge, but fools despise wisdom and discipline.

Prov. 9:10–11. The fear of the LORD is the beginning of wisdom, and knowledge of the Holy One is understanding. For through me your days will be many, and years will be added to your life.

Prov. 15:33. The fear of the LORD teaches a man wisdom, and humility comes before honor.

6. Fools despise instruction.

Prov. 1:7. The fear of the LORD is the beginning of knowledge, but fools despise wisdom and discipline.

Prov. 13:13. He who scorns instruction will pay for it, but he who respects a command is rewarded.

7. Listen to parental instruction for your own good.

Prov. 1:8–9. Listen, my son, to your father's instruction and do not forsake your mother's teaching. They will be a garland to grace your head and a chain to adorn your neck.

Prov. 4:1–4. Listen, my sons, to a father's instruction; pay attention and gain understanding. I give you sound learning, so do not forsake my teaching. When I was a boy in my father's house, still tender, and an only child of my mother, he taught me and said, "Lay hold of my words with all your heart; keep my commands and you will live."

Prov. 6:20–24. My son, keep your father's commands and do not forsake your mother's teaching. Bind them upon your heart forever; fasten them around your neck. When you walk, they will guide you; when you sleep, they will watch over you; when you awake, they will speak to you. For these commands are a lamp, this teaching is a light, and the corrections of discipline are the way to life, keeping you from the immoral woman, from the smooth tongue of the wayward wife.

8. Don't despise the Lord's discipline, for he disciplines those he loves (and parents must follow his example).

Prov. 3:11–12. My son, do not despise the LORD's discipline and do not resent his rebuke, because the LORD disciplines those he loves, as a father the son he delights in.

Heb. 12:5–11.

9. He who hates correction is stupid.

Prov. 12:1. Whoever loves discipline loves knowledge, but he who hates correction is stupid.

10. **Don't ignore discipline; be thankful for it.**

Prov. 13:18. He who ignores discipline comes to poverty and shame, but whoever heeds correction is honored.

Prov. 15:5. A fool spurns his father's discipline, but whoever heeds correction shows prudence.

Prov. 15:12. A mocker resents correction; he will not consult the wise.

Prov. 15:31–32. He who listens to a life-giving rebuke will be at home among the wise. He who ignores discipline despises himself, but whoever heeds correction gains understanding.

11. **Love requires discipline.**

Prov. 13:24. He who spares the rod hates his son, but he who loves him is careful to discipline him.

12. **If others entice you, don't consent or yield.**

Prov. 1:10–19.

Prov. 1:10. My son, if sinners entice you, do not give in to them.

Prov. 1:15. My son, do not go along with them, do not set foot on their paths.

13. **Avoid the path of the wicked; turn far from it.**

Prov. 4:14–15. Do not set foot on the path of the wicked or walk in the way of evil men. Avoid it, do not travel on it; turn from it and go on your way.

14. **Stand firm; don't be willy-nilly; don't be moved.**

1 Cor. 15:58. My dear brothers, stand firm. Let nothing move you. Always give yourselves fully to the work of the Lord, because you know that your labor in the Lord is not in vain.

15. **Be a valiant soldier of Jesus Christ; use God's armor.**

Eph. 6:10–18.

Eph. 6:10–11. Be strong in the Lord and in his mighty power. Put on the full armor of God so that you can take your stand against the devil's schemes.

16. **Joseph, the young man, stands as a good example for us.**

Gen. 39. *(Even when Joseph was far from home, a slave in Egypt, he was strong in faith and godliness. He was willing to suffer for the*

Lord, rather than to sin against him. When Potiphar's wife tempted him, he would not yield to her demands.)

Gen. 39:9–10. "How then could I do such a wicked thing and sin against God?" And though she [Potiphar's wife] spoke to Joseph day after day, he refused to go to bed with her or even be with her.

17. **Daniel also is a good example to follow. As a young man he was carried off to Babylon. There he remained faithful to God at all cost.**

    Dan. 1:8–9. Daniel resolved not to defile himself with the royal food and wine, and he asked the chief official for permission not to defile himself this way. Now God had caused the official to show favor and sympathy to Daniel. . . .

    Dan. 6. *(Even when he knew that he would be thrown into the den of lions, Daniel kept on praying to his God, against the king's decree.)*

    Dan. 6:10. Now when Daniel learned that the decree had been published, he went home to his upstairs room where the windows opened toward Jerusalem. Three times a day he got down on his knees and prayed, giving thanks to his God, just as he had done before.

18. **The three friends of Daniel also remained faithful to God at all cost.**

    Dan. 3.

    Dan. 3:16–18. Shadrach, Meshach and Abednego replied to the king, "O Nebuchadnezzar, we do not need to defend ourselves before you in this matter. If we are thrown into the blazing furnace, the God we serve is able to save us from it, and he will rescue us from your hand, O king. But even if he does not, we want you to know, O king, that we will not serve your gods or worship the image of gold you have set up."

19. **Honor your father and mother.**

    Exod. 20:12. Honor your father and mother, so that you may live long in the land the LORD your God is giving you.

20. **Honor and obey your parents.**

    Eph. 6:1–3. Children, obey your parents in the Lord, for this is right. "Honor your father and mother"—which is the first commandment with a promise—"that it may go well with you and that you may enjoy long life on the earth [Deut. 5:16]."

Col. 3:20. Children, obey your parents in everything, for this pleases the Lord.

21. Jesus was obedient to his parents.

Luke 2:51. Then he went down to Nazareth with them and was obedient to them. But his mother treasured all these things in her heart.

22. Flee the evil desires of youth.

2 Tim. 2:22. Flee the evil desires of youth, and pursue righteousness, faith, love and peace, along with those who call on the Lord out of a pure heart.